THE STORY
OF
DISCIPLESHIP

CHRIST, HUMANITY, AND CHURCH IN NARRATIVE PERSPECTIVE

Elizabeth Barnes

ABINGDON PRESS
Nashville

THE STORY OF DISCIPLESHIP:
CHRIST, HUMANITY, AND CHURCH IN NARRATIVE PERSPECTIVE

Copyright © 1995 by Abingdon Press

95 96 97 98 99 00 01 02 03 04— 10 9 8 7 6 5 4 3 2 1

Library of Congress Cataloging-in-Publication Data

Barnes, Elizabeth B.
    The story of discipleship: Christ, humanity, and church in narrative perspective / Elizabeth Barnes.
        p.   cm.
    Includes bibliographical references (pp. 173-76).
    ISBN 0-687-396573
       1. Identification (Religion) 2. Storytelling—Religious aspects—Christianity. 3. Christian life—Baptist authors. I. Title.
BV4509.5/B374   1995   95-1072
230'.046—dc20   CIP

Scripture quotations, unless otherwise noted, are from the New Revised Standard Version Bible, Copyright © 1989 by the Division of Christian Education of the National Council of Churches of Christ in the USA. Used by permission.

Excerpts from "A Good Man is Hard to Find" in *A Good Man is Hard to find and Other Stories*, copyright © 1953 by Flannery O'Connor and renewed 1981 by Regina O'Connor, reprinted by permission of Harcourt Brace and Company.

Excerpts from *The Grapes of Wrath* by John Steinbeck. Copyright 1939, renewed © 1967 by John Steinbeck Used by permission of Viking Penguin, a division of Penguin Books USA Inc.

Excerpts from *Babette's Feast and the Anecdotes of Destiny* by Isak Dinesen. Copyright © 1953, 1958 and renewed 1981, 1986 by Isak Dinesen. Reprinted by permission of Random House, Inc.

Excerpts from *Out of Africa* by Isak Dinesen. Copyright © 1937 by Random House, Inc. Copyright © renewed 1965 by Rungstedlundfonden. Reprinted by permission of Random House, Inc.

The story selection on pages 119-21 is reprinted, with permission, from *Storytelling: Imagination and Faith*, copyright © 1984 by William J. Bausch (paper, 232 pp., $9.95), published by Twenty-Third Publications, P.O. Box 180, Mystic, CT 06335. Toll free: 1-800-321-0411.

Excerpts from *Jesus Christ: Resurrection* by Douglas E. Wingeier, (pp. 36, 37, 42, 43). Copyright © 1985 by Graded Press. Used by permission.

Printed in the United States of America on recycled, acid-free paper.

to my daughters and son

ANNE ELIZABETH BARNES
REBEKAH ELLEN BARNES
LALON LEM BARNES, III

with love and hope of honoring them

CONTENTS

ACKNOWLEDGMENTS

There are so many people, not all of whom I shall remember to mention, who have enabled the undertaking and completion of this work. A few, however, deserve special recognition and thanks. Among those are James Wm. McClendon, Jr., Stanley Hauerwas, Bob Osborn, Frederick Herzog, and Richard Hester, who read the manuscript at an early stage of its development and gave valuable critique and encouragement.

I am particularly grateful to James Wm. McClendon, Jr. for the experience of working with him as he wrote the *Doctrine* volume of his systematic theology. That experience helped to shape much of what appears now in this effort to examine the doctrines of Christ, humanity, and church from a narrative perspective.

Special gratitude is extended to my editor, Bob Ratcliff, first, for his interest in this project, and second, for the expertise, work, and wisdom he offered to secure its development and completion.

Linda McNally, faculty secretary at Baptist Theological Seminary at Richmond, gave cheerful and valuable assistance in getting the manuscript into acceptable WordPerfect form; for this I am grateful to Linda.

John William Eddins, Jr. my husband and theological companion, encouraged, corrected, inspired, and supported me and this work itself. To John, especially, I am thankful for transforming what otherwise would have been a lonely, though valuable, task into one of shared and happy companionship.

Many students, kinfolk, and friends, in various ways enabled the writing of this book. I wish I could name each one, for each made a distinct and valuable contribution. I give to all my thanks.

Elizabeth Barnes
August 1, 1994

INTRODUCTION

In this book, I shall apply a narrative methodology which I have been working on for some years now. Basic to this perspective is the presupposition that story is primary. I agree with George Lindbeck that Christians are persons who have been shaped by the stories of Israel, Jesus, and the church (Lindbeck, 1984). I agree, too, with James McClendon that this storied tradition is currently present in the life of the church; as McClendon puts it, "this is that," meaning that the "this" of the church's story now stands in essential continuity with the ""that" of the biblical story (McClendon, 1986).

Neither Lindbeck nor McClendon, as well as other narrativists asking similar questions, however, ask clearly enough *how* the stories of Israel, Jesus, and the church shape us—how it comes to be that "this is that." My own long-considered answer is: they shape us and "this becomes that" through *interlacing*. Biblical stories and contemporary stories interlace. This has always been true for Christians, and while it happens more effectively, perhaps, if we are conscious and intentional about the interlacing, it happens whether we are altogether conscious of it or not. Furthermore, *scripture's authority resides in its power to interlace creatively and redemptively with all our other stories.* Through interlacing with our many other stories, biblical stories *function normatively*. I shall say it another way: biblical stories are normative precisely because they interlace with our other stories in a way that makes the biblical texts authoritatively functional as shapers of us and our view of the world. It is in this way that Christians can speak of the Bible as God's Word and as God's *living* Word. Scripture's liveliness inheres in its interlacing genius. *The power of the Spirit is the power to interlace the biblical narratives with humankind's multitudinous narratives so that transformation occurs and a true story is told.*

Interlacing is artistic. It is a kind of dance. It is a kind of artistic weave, a back-and-forth movement *like* that of the dance or the weaver's shuttle, joining biblical narratives and other narratives, now giving, now taking, interlocking, mutually enriching and expanding each the other. Mystery, surprise, delight, creation and re-creation; all these and more emerge as the interlacing proceeds.

The proper work of theology, I propose, is *participation in and reflection on this weave of interlacing stories* and its meaning for doctrine. According to the thesis of this study, Christology, anthropology, and ecclesiology are given to us through the interlacing of biblical stories and other stories, thereby rendering the identity of Christ to us and, secondarily, the identity of ourselves to us, as well.

Like James McClendon, I am a Baptist theologian writing from within the experience of Christian community as free church believers have lived it. Informed by McClendon's baptist vision (small *b* to include those believers church Christians who do not call themselves Baptists), this work stands in the line of the baptist tradition and is my contribution to its continuing dialogue of faith with other Christians and those outside the Christian camp, as well.

The methodology which I am setting forth and recommending has to do with examining stories, biblical and otherwise. The biblical stories we shall examine we first heard in Sunday School, Sunday morning worship, and Vacation Bible School. We also saw these stories enacted in baptism and the Lord's Supper, and we ourselves entered the stories with our own baptism and communion at the Lord's Table. As Lindbeck suggests, we entered the biblical text and began to live as characters in the Jesus Story, a phenomenon to which he refers as intratextuality. In theological reflection now, we remember those formative Sundays and summer Bible Schools. Through worship and discipleship, crucial connecting links between the Bible stories and all our other stories, we continue the process, a process of memory, worship, and reflection. We remember and, in so doing, tell ourselves and one another the stories again. And we interlace them again.

Thus far, all that I have said has been hopeful and optimistic, even confident, regarding the process of "this is that," wherein the world of the Bible becomes ours and we become present-day characters in the Jesus Story. Now, I must admit it is not all so easy and simple. The short stories of Flannery O'Connor and Dan Via's observations on them have helped me to see that Lindbeck's notion of intratextuality and McClendon's idea of "this is that" and the contemporaneity of scripture fail to consider soberly enough the fact that often, very often, it just does not happen. The stories of Israel, Jesus, and the church remain distant, frozen, remote, sterile for contemporary people. "This" does not become "that"; the distant past remains distant and non-conversant with present-day strugglers and their problems. The reasons for this failure of biblical stories to interlace transformatively with contemporary stories are many and complex. For one thing, preachers, Sunday School teachers, and other Christians are not always good storytellers. Second, forces within the personal lives of those storytellers may hinder the receiving and telling of a true story. Third, social and cultural forces can do the same thing. In addition, hearers throw up their own psychic and intellectual blocks oftentimes. No doubt, there are other reasons accounting for this ubiquitous problem.

Those reasons and influences mean that interlacing can fail to happen. Or, it can happen in a skewed and distorted way, cutting the nerve of the true story of God's grace, or even twisting it into a grotesque caricature, thereby rendering grace's reception ineffectual, even false, in the resulting story which emerges. O'Connor's short story, "A Good Man Is Hard to Find," offers a look at the failure of authentic interlacing to occur. "This" has not become "that" for The Misfit in O'Connor's narrative. He has heard the Jesus Story, but it has been badly told—and lived, we can surmise. The grandmother whose life is about to end at the point of The Misfit's gun has received and transmitted the Story poorly, as well. The consequences are tragic for all the characters in the narrative.

> She wanted to tell him that he must pray. She opened and closed her mouth several times before anything came out. Finally she found herself saying, "Jesus, Jesus," meaning, Jesus will help you, but the way she was saying it, it sounded as if she might be cursing.
> "Yes'm," The Misfit said as if he agreed. "Jesus thrown everything off balance. . . ."

11

There were two more pistol reports and the grandmother raised her head like a parched old turkey hen crying for water and called, "Bailey Boy, Bailey Boy!" as if her heart would break.

"Jesus was the only One that ever raised the dead." The Misfit continued, "and He shouldn't have done it. He thrown everything off balance. If He did what He said, then it's nothing for you to do but throw away everything and follow Him, and if He didn't, then it's nothing for you to do but enjoy the few minutes you got left the best way you can—by killing somebody or burning down his house or doing some other meanness to him. No pleasure but meanness," he said and his voice had become almost a snarl.

"Maybe He didn't raise the dead," the old lady mumbled, not knowing what she was saying and feeling so dizzy that she sank down in the ditch with her legs twisted under her.

"I wasn't there so I can't say He didn't," The Misfit said. "I wisht I had of been there," he said, hitting the ground with his fist. "*It ain't right I wasn't there because if I had of been there I would of known. Listen lady,*" he said in a high voice, "*if I had of been there I would of known and I wouldn't be like I am now.*" His voice seemed about to crack and the man's face twisted close to her own as if he were going to cry and she murmured, "why you're one of my babies. You're one of my own children!" She reached out and touched him on the shoulder. The Misfit sprang back as if a snake had bitten him and shot her three times through the chest. Then he put his gun down on the ground and took off his glasses and began to clean them.

Hiram and Bobby Lee returned from the woods and stood over the ditch, looking down at the grandmother who half sat and half lay in a puddle of blood with her legs crossed under her like a child's and her face smiling up at the cloudless sky.

Without his glasses, The Misfit's eyes were red-rimmed and pale and defenseless-looking. "Take her off and throw her where you thrown the others," he said, picking up the cat that was rubbing itself against his leg.

"She was a talker, wasn't she?" Bobby Lee said, sliding down the ditch with a yodel.

"She would of been a good woman," The Misfit said, "if it had been somebody there to shoot her every minute of her life."

"Some fun!" Bobby Lee said.

"Shut up, Bobby Lee," The Misfit said. "It's no real pleasure in life." (O'Connor, 1946/1989:131–33, emphasis added)

For The Misfit, Jesus is a stranger locked in a distant past. He wishes that he could have been there. He believes that he would have been different if he had. Dan Via has challenged The Misfit's assumption, pointing out that Jesus' contemporaries, including his disciples, had trouble understanding Jesus (Via, 1991: unpublished lecture). This fact implies that, whether in the first Christian century or on the eve of the third Christian millennium, the Story becomes true and truly one's own through a complex process which we have not clearly identified and articulated for ourselves and others. Does "this become that," as Via points out some students of O'Connor's suggest she believes, only after a *violent* event cleaves a passage through which grace can travel? It seems to me that this notion is going too far and discounts evidence to the contrary. It is said that O'Connor once reported that she never let the word "beauty" cross her lips. Did she thereby shut herself off (protecting herself from what perceived threat?) from grace which comes through the beautiful and gently good? In any case, O'Connor's gripping story serves to jolt us out of our self-congratulatory temptation to deceive ourselves about the way the gospel becomes good news for new disciples in new generations. "This" becomes "that" neither so automatically nor so often as we might have slipped into thinking it does or wished that it did.

An easy, too facile interpretation of how the gospel Story becomes truly the story of those who hear its proclamation and join the community of believers as one of its number has resulted in error and sometimes, as O'Connor's story reminds us, in tragedy. Focusing again on another of the church's primary doctrinal affirmations can help us both to see the extent of that self-deception and to correct its distorting influence. The doctrine of original sin has functioned, when functioning best, in just this corrective way. The Christian theologian does not have to interpret the teaching of original sin precisely as Augustine conceptualized it to acknowledge its validity and indispensable place in Christian doctrine. Augustine's notion that all humankind enters the world stained already by sexual conception and seminal origination can be, and needs to be, rejected while more profound aspects of this great thinker's ideas still serve to guide our reflection. That human beings still, even after redemption from the guilt of their sin, have a bent toward rebellion and the self-deception accompanying that ubiquitous sinning is as convincing theologically today as when Augustine formulated that notion for the church. Therefore, affirmations that "this becomes that" truly and effectively must take into full account the sobering reality that original sin, one's own and others', often distorts and even subverts that event. Such is evidently what had happened in regard to The Misfit in O'Connor's story. He had heard the Jesus Story and knew it well enough to have reflected on its implications for human life generally and his own particularly. Furthermore, he knew how to assess a genuine Christian witness; that the grandmother's was not such a true witness he readily saw. He also knew when, in her terror, the old woman flashed a response of faithful Christian sensitivity and conviction, but that pitifully delayed fidelity had not characterized her life, and it was too late. The Misfit's reply to his cohort tells the story: "'She would of been a good woman,' The Misfit said, 'if it had been somebody there to shoot her every minute of her life!'" The Misfit has lived in a culture which has preached Jesus and failed to live his story truly. His own life has suffered the destructive consequences of having been simultaneously preached at and rejected by the proclaimers of *agape*. Original sin's ineffaceable mark dialectically joins the good news of the kerygma. This dialectical negative fact of original sin must be recognized in our positive formulations of the true, but not absolute and invulnerable, fact that the gospel Story becomes the true story of new generations. A balanced theology will take care to incorporate that recognition.

But "this" *does* become "that," and when it does, all reality is re-ordered and reinterpreted. When it does happen, it happens through a marvelous and mysterious interlacing of stories, continuing the Story, adding new characters in new settings, developing the plot according to God's still-unfolding narrative.

Let us summarize: "This" becomes "that" by interlacing, through the interlacing of normative biblical stories and other stories which, *with* the stories of our faith, shape us as the people we are. Interlacing happens all the time; it is the means by which we make sense of the world. Interlacing happens consciously, semi-consciously, and unconsciously. Waking and dreaming, we interlace stories. *The church's best theological work can be done, I propose, when we intentionally interlace our normative biblical narra-*

tives with other narratives in the context of worship and discipleship, reflecting carefully and rigorously on the dividend.

Let us look further at McClendon's insights. McClendon points out in his lectures and writing that "this is that" is the scripture writers' own theological method. They and the characters they write about understand and express God's relations to humanity and world by understanding past biblical narratives as present in their own experience. We see Jesus himself doing this in his words to the hometown folk in the synagogue at Nazareth. The story of the suffering servant in Isaiah is his own story; "this is that." Jesus' followers and Luke do the same in the Pentecost narrative in Acts. Joel's story in the Hebrew Bible is their story, too. They are the sons and daughters who now are seeing new visions and dreaming new dreams.

Our challenge is to appropriate the biblical theologians' pregnant method and develop it for today. This is what I am trying to do. We have some new stories they did not have. They had some which no longer function and some which are lost to us. Interlaced with our stories today, however, the biblical stories can do for us what they have done for Christians before us: they can transform our lives, making us faithful and true characters in God's on-going narrative of grace and peace.

In this book, I shall proceed, then, upon the following presuppositions:

1. Biblical stories are normative for Christians and the church.
2. Biblical stories function normatively by interlacing with our many other stories *creatively* and *redemptively*.
3. The Bible's authority resides in its power to interlace with our diverse stories in ways that challenge our errors, correct our distortions, and transform and complete our unfinished narratives as stories of love, justice, and peace.
4. Worship and discipleship function as connecting links between the biblical stories and our other narratives, facilitating the work of interlacing and acting as ecclesiastical self-critical elements in the interlacing process.

Part I will focus on the Jesus Story, interlacing the biblical narratives with various other stories and focusing special emphasis on the work of Isak Dinesen and her short story *Babette's Feast*, in particular. Part II will move our focus from Christology to anthropology and interlace biblical stories with stories of human conflict as we look at what William Faulkner described as the "problems of the human heart in conflict with itself." In Part III, we shall turn our attention to stories of hope, renewal, and resurrection, bringing together the stories of Jesus and the stories of humankind's struggles with its conflicted heart with other biblical narratives of God's world house and divine hospitality. There, we shall interlace scriptural narratives with stories of worship and discipleship as told in Christian lives and through other narrative modes.

PART I

The Jesus Story

The Jesus Story is the central one, is it not? What so captivates us about this story and the smaller stories within it? What keeps us coming back to it and them? Why and how does the story of Jesus function as the story that shapes us as people who call ourselves Christians? In what way is the story of Jesus of Nazareth both the story of God and the story of humankind? How is the Jesus Story the story of Incarnation? Our investigation in the following pages will help to answer these questions, at least in part.

In the midst of the war in the Persian Gulf, I was convinced and remain so that the Jesus Story is a peace story. It is about a man who counseled turning the other cheek to the one who has already struck us, loving the enemy, giving both coat and cloak to the assailant. What kind of story is this? We have never been comfortable with it, and it is not hard to see why. The Jesus Story is about a person who refused to fight either for Israel or to protect himself. Instead, he submitted to a humiliating and inhumane crucifixion on a cross. He blessed the peacemakers and called them the daughters and sons of God. These, he claimed, along with the meek and mild, would inhabit God's house and enjoy God's commonwealth, not the wealthy status-seekers who tore down barns to build bigger ones, or clothed themselves in fine linens and purple, or stole from the widows and fatherless or taxed the poor beyond their means to subsist. Those who did these things, Jesus said, would dwell in a lake of fire—a rather graphic image!

The French-Canadian movie *Jesus of Montreal* raises the question of what happens when a person becomes a disciple and truly begins to live the Jesus Story, telling it through her own story, continuing, as it were, the incarnation. Daniel Coulombe is a young actor who becomes such a disciple and finds that the ending of the story is the same for him as for Jesus—rejection, persecution, and finally, death. Yet Daniel's story also tells us that life is more and other than waiting for the end, getting by, self-delusion, and hypocrisy. In the film, a Catholic priest functions as Daniel's counter-image. This priest, too, had wanted to be an actor, but lacking the courage to pursue that dream, he had entered the priesthood with the approval of his family and community, and at least, as he put it, had the opportunity to travel and see many of the world's great dramatic productions. Now he is sexually involved with a female actor and lives a secret life, holding on to his status and creature comforts. Unable to renounce his security, even though his lover pleads with him to live openly as the person he truly is and offers him a home with her and the chance to live without secrets, the priest becomes an agent, not only of his own destruction, but of Daniel's, as well. The silver cross on his lapel is a silent, mocking caricature, a travesty of the cross under which Daniel is finally crushed.

Jesus of Montreal, like the biblical stories themselves, shocks us with its probity. Living the Jesus Story means pulling out the stops, this film suggests. It means giving up security, wealth, and acclaim for the single worthwhile thing—a true story, a journey to the story-formed self which, truly taken, is a journey to God and others. Because the priest in *Jesus of Montreal* chooses to live a story which is not his own, his life is a pretense. Alienated from himself and self-deceived, he is unable to relate intimately with others. For that reason he substitutes sex for intimacy. His empty cathedral is a silent mirror of the emptiness within himself, his own empty soul. A victim of self-deception, he half-believes the lie he lives.

In the film, five young actors are hired to update and present a forty-year-old religious pageant at a local Roman Catholic church. They are given access to current research, and Daniel, the actor portraying Jesus, conducts further research of his own in the city library. While he is there, a librarian asks, "Are you looking for Jesus? He will find you."

This is precisely what happens. As Daniel enacts the role, he is found by the Jesus Story and begins to take his place within it. Furthermore, this process occurs as a communal reality; Daniel becomes a disciple as he lives the story in company with others

18

whose welfare grows increasingly more important to him. For them, and for his truest self, he is ready to live the story to its tragic conclusion.

Daniel Coulombe's story provides an example of George Lindbeck's contention that Christians become so *intratextually.* Lindbeck's important book *The Nature of Doctrine* focused the theological world's attention on the process whereby Christians become Christian. Christians learn the story of Israel, Jesus, and the church well enough that it becomes their story. The Christian story explains the world and orients the Christian's understanding of self and all other reality in terms of the story itself (Lindbeck, 1984). In *Revelation and Theology,* Ronald Thiemann makes a similar point with the aid of Matthias Grünewald's painting *The Crucifixion* (Thiemann, 1985/1987). This famous work depicts the crucifixion scene with an empty spot directly at the foot of the cross, left there for the viewer to enter and join the other worshipers in the painting. This painting, Thiemann points out, captures the spirit of Lindbeck's notion of intratextuality. The hearer or reader of the story is drawn inside the text and begins to live the story as a modern-day disciple. Daniel Coulombe, in *Jesus of Montreal,* experiences essentially this very reality. He finally is killed because he dares to interpret and live the story in all its radical extravagance.

Interlacing the Jesus Story and *Jesus of Montreal* can open lenses for a clearer and contemporary focus on the nature of the Christian life lived in modern circumstances and in faithfulness to the Story itself. Like Daniel Coulombe, present-day characters in the Christian story see in the story of Jesus that they can expect to encounter misunderstanding, opposition, and resistance to the truth-telling which their commitment entails. Yet there is a happy side: like Daniel, they can also expect to discover their true selves in the living of the Story and resolute energy for carrying on that Christian life. Juxtaposing Jesus of Nazareth and "Jesus" of Montreal moves the Story's setting to twentieth-century Western life and culture and unfolds its plot in modern religious, social, and political systems and events. The gospel Story consequently takes on jolting contemporaneity and the film story acts as revelatory grid for a new telling of the Jesus Story for Christians and non-Christians alike. As Christians do the work of interlacing in the context of worship and discipleship, the interlaced stories can illumine, engage, and energize them for their work of worship, witness, and discipleship.

While Christ-themes have multiplied in film, they have diminished in the classical artistic media of painting, sculpture, and music. However, as in the newer medium of film, the literary arts experienced a resurgence of Christ-themes even before that in film. Rose of Sharon in John Steinbeck's *The Grapes of Wrath* is a compelling Christ figure. Her story is a story of the poor, the oppressed. Having been abandoned by her husband, delivered a stillborn baby, and nearly lost her own life from starvation, Rose gives her dead baby's milk to save a dying stranger. Steinbeck's final scene is one of the most powerful in American literature:

> Ma walked to the corner and looked down at the man. He was about fifty, his whiskery face gaunt, and his open eyes were vague and staring. The boy stood beside her. "Your pa?" Ma asked.
>
> "Yeah! Says he wasn't hungry, or he jus' et. Give me the food. Now he's too weak. Can't hardly move."
>
> The pounding of the rain decreased to a soothing swish on the roof. The gaunt man moved his lips. Ma knelt beside him and put her ear close. His lips moved again.
>
> "Sure," Ma said. "You jus' be easy. He'll be awright. You jus' wait'll I get them wet clo'es off'n my girl."
>
> Ma went back to the girl. "Now slip 'em off," she said. She held the comfort up to screen her from view. And when she was naked, Ma folded the comfort about her.
>
> The boy was at her side again explaining, "I didn' know. He said he et, or he wasn't hungry. Las' night I went an' bust a winda an' stoled some bread. Made 'im chew 'er down. But he puked it all up, an' then he was weaker. Got to have soup or milk. You folks got money to git milk?"
>
> Ma said, "Hush. Don' worry. We'll figger somepin out."
>
> Suddenly the boy cried, "He's dyin', I tell you! He's starvin' to death, I tell you."
>
> "Hush," said Ma. She looked at Pa and Uncle John standing helplessly gazing at the sick man. She looked at Rose of Sharon huddled in the comfort. Ma's eyes passed Rose of Sharon's eyes, and then came back to them. And the two women looked deep into each other. The girl's breath came short and gasping.
>
> She said, "Yes."
>
> Ma smiled. "I knowed you would. I knowed!" She looked down at her hands, tight-locked in her lap.

Rose of Sharon whispered, "Will-will you all—go out?" The rain whisked lightly on the roof.

Ma leaned forward and with her palm she brushed the tousled hair back from her daughter's forehead, and she kissed her on the forehead. Ma got up quickly. "Come on you fellas," she called. "You come out in the tool shed."

Ruthie opened her mouth to speak. "Hush," Ma said. "Hush and git." She herded them through the door, drew the boy with her; and she closed the squeaking door.

For a minute Rose of Sharon sat still in the whispering barn. Then she hoisted her tired body up and drew the comfort about her. She moved slowly to the corner and stood looking down at the wasted face, into the wide, frightened eyes. Then slowly she lay down beside him. He shook his head slowly from side to side. Rose of Sharon loosened one side of the blanket and bared her breast. "You got to," she said. She squirmed closer and pulled his head close. "There!" she said. "There." Her hand moved gently in his hair. She looked up and across the barn, and her lips came together and smiled mysteriously. (Steinbeck, 1939/1976:579–81)

The Joads, the central characters in *The Grapes of Wrath*, are a religious family, depending on the community and aid of poor Christians like themselves for survival and extending the same to others. Steinbeck concludes his novel with the story of their daughter's sacrifice. They had chosen her name from a favorite hymn of the poor about Jesus. She, like Jesus himself, is the Rose of Sharon, sacrificing herself for a suffering fellow human. Steinbeck's feminine Christ is one of the most convincing images in contemporary literature.

Both *Jesus of Montreal* and *The Grapes of Wrath* are stories of self-sacrifice informed and shaped by the Christian story. As such, they interlace with the biblical narratives of Jesus' own self-sacrifice and open windows on those stories, even as the biblical narratives open windows on them and correct and expand their meaning. Christians interlace these literary and scriptural stories with their church and personal stories, creating a productive, complex weave in which Christ, humanity, and church are understood.

A primary story is Isak Dinesen's masterpiece, *Babette's Feast*. Like *Jesus of Montreal* and *The Grapes of Wrath*, *Babette's Feast* is shaped by the Christian story and constitutes a contemporary interpretation of it.

The Christ image in Dinesen's story is an unlikely one. We are unaccustomed to thinking in Dinesen's terms. But making the effort can open up the gospel narratives in unanticipated and surprising ways. An examination of *Babette's Feast* will interlace with the Jesus Story to our astonishment and gain. Let us get the narrative before us.

Dinesen's story is set in Norway and spans half a century before and following the conflict surrounding the Paris Commune of 1870. Martine and Philippa, named for Martin Luther and Philip Melanchthon, are the unmarried, devoted daughters of a deceased "Dean and a prophet, the founder of a pious ecclesiastic party or sect" within the Lutheran persuasion (Dinesen, 1953/1988:3). Central to this religious community's perspective is a rejection of all earthly pleasures. These good folk deny the self and believe that theirs is a faithful model for Christian self-sacrifice.

Because self-sacrifice is the guiding image for these believers, both Martine and Philippa had renounced their opportunity to marry as young women and devoted themselves to their father and the poor to whom they ministered. As women approaching middle age now and with their father dead, Martine and Philippa endeavor to carry on his life's work.

Fifteen years before the main action of the story Martine and Philippa had spurned nuptial love and the fulfillment of marriage in favor of "an ideal of heavenly love" which they had been taught to seek: "they were all filled with it and did not let themselves be touched by the flames of this world" (Dinesen, 1953/1988:5). For Martine and Philippa this heavenly love was separated from that love which comes through earthly channels.

A young lieutenant had sought to win Martine's heart. Too young to court her with confidence, Lieutenant Lorens Loewenhielm was further dismayed by Martine's failure to encourage his efforts. In frustration he left, resolving to distinguish himself in his career "and the day was to come when he would cut a brilliant figure in a brilliant world," a phrase which wryly indicates the emptiness and lack of satisfaction the young lieutenant would find there. All the while, "In the yellow house of Berlevaag, Philippa sometimes turned the talk to the handsome, silent young man who had so suddenly made his appearance, and so suddenly disappeared again. Her elder sister would then answer her gently, with a still, clear face, and find other things to discuss" (Dinesen, 1953/1988:8).

Philippa's own story of loss is perhaps even more poignant, if not tragic. Gifted with a magnificent singing voice, she had won the heart of one Achille Papin, an outstanding tenor from Paris who visited their small church and heard her sing. Recognizing musical genius when he heard it, Papin appropriately and prayerfully acknowledged its source: "'Almighty God,' he thought, 'Thy power is without end, and Thy mercy reacheth into the clouds! And here is a prima donna of the opera who will lay Paris at her feet'" (Dinesen, 1953/1988:9). Wishing to enable Philippa to give her extraordinary gift to the world, Papin delighted, as well, in the prospect of their singing together. Such a splendid partner would open for him the yet unfurled wings of his own great talent, and they would soar together. "I have been wrong in believing that I was growing old. My greatest triumphs are before me! The world will once more believe in miracles when she and I sing together!" (Dinesen, 1953/1988:10).

When Philippa began to feel the romantic attraction between them, however, she terminated her singing lessons with Monsieur Papin and refused to see him. Philippa's gift was withheld. The world would not be comforted and made happier by her incredibly beautiful soprano. Although with it she could have, as Papin observed, brought "consolation and strength to the wronged and oppressed," Philippa would continue to sing only for the few souls who attended their small church. Papin's own hopes were crushed as well. "Never again shall I be the divine Papin. And this poor weedy garden of the world has lost its nightingale!" Concerning Papin, Dinesen comments, "Achille Papin took the first boat from Berlevaag. Of this visitor from the great world the sisters spoke but little; they lacked the words with which to discuss him." (Dinesen, 1953/1988:12).

Fifteen years later, Babette arrives. Having escaped the defeat of the Paris Commune, though not before losing her husband and son in that conflict, Babette seeks refuge and livelihood with the Dean's daughters as their cook. What she does not tell them is of her great renown as a French chef. Dinesen foreshadows what is to come and suggests the redemptive, christic role Babette will play: "the true reason for Babette's presence in the two sisters' house was to be found further back in time and *deeper down in the*

23

domain of human hearts" (Dinesen, 1953/1988:4, emphasis added). Babette brings with her a letter of recommendation from Achille Papin. At the end of his letter, he addresses Philippa directly:

> For fifteen years, Miss Philippa, I have grieved that your voice should never fill the Grand Opera of Paris. . . . And, yet, my lost Zerlina, and yet, soprano of the snow! As I write this I feel that the grave is not the end. In Paradise I shall hear your voice again. There you will sing, without fears or scruples, as God meant you to sing. There you will be the great artist that God meant you to be. Ah! how you will enchant the angels. (Dinesen, 1953/1988:14)

And then, with marvelous terseness and colossal understatement, Dinesen has Papin write: "Babette can cook" (Dinesen, 1953/1988:14).

Isak Dinesen deserves her reputation as storyteller extraordinaire for the timing and subtle genius encapsulated in those three words: "Babette can cook." Philippa must await paradise to enchant the angels; with three words, Dinesen foretells Babette's own paradisal gift and its enchantment of mortals.

Immediately, Babette's presence transforms the sisters' meager household. "She had appeared to be a beggar; she turned out to be a conqueror. Her quiet countenance and her steady, deep glance had magnetic qualities; under her eyes things moved, noiselessly, into their proper places" (Dinesen, 1953/1988:15). Missing the significance of Babette's self-possession and strength, the sisters resolve, good Christians as they are, to set for her an example that will lead to her conversion. They begin with food.

> The first day after Babette had entered their service they took her before them and explained to her that they were poor and that to them luxurious fare was sinful. Their own food must be as plain as possible; it was the soup-pails and baskets for their poor that signified. Babette nodded her head; as a girl, she informed her ladies, she had been cook to an old priest who was a saint. Upon this the sisters resolved to surpass the French priest in asceticism. (Dinesen, 1953/1988:16)

With characteristic restraint, Dinesen leaves her reader to fill in the blanks. What was the specific nature of the old priest's saintliness? Asceticism? Or something else?

From the beginning of her tenure with the sisters, Babette distinguishes herself as an assertive and thrifty bargainer in the marketplace: "she beat down the prices of Berlevaag's flintiest tradesmen," a cook whose modest soup-pails and baskets nonetheless "acquired a new, mysterious power to stimulate and strengthen their poor and sick," and a beneficent presence to the old Sisters and Brothers of the sect. Employing religious allusion to Christ, Dinesen says of Babette: "The stone which the builders had almost refused had become the headstone of the corner" (Dinesen, 1953/1988:17).

Martine's and Philippa's are not the only diminished and truncated lives in the small Brotherhood. Old rancors, trespasses unforgiven, guilts still festering, and other resentments plague the aging Brothers and Sisters of the flock.

> There were in the congregation two old women who before their conversion had spread slander upon each other, and thereby to each other ruined a marriage and an inheritance. Today they could not remember happenings of yesterday or a week ago, but they remembered this forty-year-old wrong and kept going through the ancient accounts; they scowled at each other. There was an old Brother who suddenly called to mind how another Brother, forty-five years ago, had cheated him in a deal; he could have wished to dismiss the matter from his mind, but it stuck there like a deep-seated, festering splinter. There was a gray, honest skipper and a furrowed, pious widow, who in their young days, while she was the wife of another man, had been sweethearts. Of late each had begun to grieve, while shifting the burden of guilt from his own shoulders to those of the other and back again, and to worry about the possible terrible consequences, through all eternity, to himself, brought upon him by one who had pretended to hold him dear. They grew pale at the meetings in the yellow house and avoided each other's eyes. (Dinesen, 1953/1988:19,20)

The beliefs and practices of these Brothers' and Sisters' religious community had failed to enable them to forgive others or themselves. Renouncing the pleasures of the world had been ineffectual in softening the heart. It is into this situation that Babette's good fortune is introduced. With it, Babette will change the lives of these elderly friends for whom she has already been a transforming presence.

Winning ten thousand francs in the French lottery, Babette asks leave to prepare a banquet for the Brotherhood in commemoration of the anniversary of the Dean's hundredth birthday.

Accustomed to giving and uncomfortable with receiving, Martine and Philippa disapprove of the money's origin, are repelled by the idea of indulging in lavish fare, and unable to receive such an expensive gift for themselves. They deny her request. It is at this point that Dinesen introduces an uncommon understanding of prayer. Babette appeals:

> Ladies, you who say your prayers every day, can you imagine what it means to a human heart to have no prayer to make? What would Babette have had to pray for? Nothing! Tonight she had a prayer to make, from the bottom of her heart. Do you not then feel tonight, my ladies, that it becomes you to grant it her, with such joy as that with which the good God has granted you your own? (Dinesen, 1953/1988:23)

This notion of prayer completely flies over their heads. Babette's request is an implied prayer that she might conform her plans and efforts to the outstanding culinary gift which God has given her and thus join it to God's loving and creative intentions for the community around them and of which they are members. Only later will some beginning intimation of Babette's meaning break through to them. The sisters are still uncertain, but because she has heretofore asked so little in the way of favors, Babette is granted her request.

> Their consent in the end completely changed Babette. They saw that as a young woman she had been beautiful. And they wondered whether in this hour they themselves had not, for the very first time, become to her the 'good people' of Achille Papin's letter. (Dinesen, 1953/1988:24)

Babette's physical beauty is allowed to shine in the prospect of expressing her art. The sisters, in turn, become "good people" in agreeing to become the recipients of that art.

But the sisters have a long history of denying the joys of the flesh. When the food-stuffs and goods that Babette has ordered arrive, Martine is apprehensive:

> In the light of the lamp it looked like some greenish-black stone, but when set down on the kitchen floor it suddenly shot out a snake-like head and moved it slightly from side to side. Martine had seen pictures of tortoises, and had even as a child owned a pet tortoise, but this thing was monstrous in size and terrible to behold. She backed out of the kitchen without a word.

She dared not tell her sister what she had seen. She passed an almost sleepless night; she thought of her father and felt that on his very birthday she and her sister were lending his house to a witches' sabbath. When at last she fell asleep she had a terrible dream, in which she saw Babette poisoning the old Brothers and Sisters, Philippa and herself. (Dinesen, 1953/1988:26)

We might ask what it is that Martine fears Babette will kill in her and the others. Dinesen's story promises to show us, and it does it in wonderfully subtle and marvelously nuanced manner.

The night of the banquet arrives. Having covenanted with one another to protect themselves from Babette's sorcery by saying not a word about the food and closing themselves off from the temptation of the senses, the old Brothers and Sisters gather with Martine and Philippa for Babette's feast, all of them quaking with apprehension. ". . . .we will cleanse our tongues of all taste and purify them of all delight or disgust of the senses, keeping and preserving them for the higher things of praise and thanksgiving" (Dinesen, 1953/1988:27).

Enter Lorens Loewenhielm, now General Loewenhielm, no longer the awkward, self-conscious, young lieutenant who thirty years ago despaired of happiness with Martine. He is visiting for the first time since his departure so long ago, having come to see his aunt, a member of the sect, who "begged permission to bring him with her. It would do him good, for the dear boy seemed to be in somewhat low spirits" (Dinesen, 1953/1988:28). His youthful dream of glory has been realized: "General Loewenhielm had obtained everything that he had striven for in life and was admired and envied by everyone." However, "Something was wrong, somewhere, and he carefully felt his mental self all over, as one feels a finger over to determine the place of a deep-seated, invisible thorn" (Dinesen, 1953/1988:31).

General Loewenhielm decides to return to Berlevaag and the house of the sisters to prove to himself that he had made the right choice three decades ago. He feels sure that, "The low rooms, the haddock and the glass of water on the table before him should all be called in to bear evidence that in their milieu the existence of Lorens Loewenhielm would very soon have become sheer misery" (Dinesen, 1953/1988:33).

Babette's feast begins: Turtle-soup, Blinis Demidoff, Veuve

Cliquot 1860, peaches, grapes, figs, and finally, Cailles en Sarco-phage. The General remembers a dinner in Paris at the celebrated Café Anglais many years ago:

> An incredibly recherché and palatable dish had been served there; he had asked its name from his fellow diner, Colonel Galliffet, and the Colonel had smilingly told him that it was named "Cailles en Sarcophage." He had further told him that the dish had been invented by the chef of the very café in which they were dining, a person known all over Paris as the greatest culinary genius of the age, and—most surprisingly—a woman! "And indeed," said Colo-nel Galliffet, "this woman is now turning a dinner at the Café Anglais into a kind of love affair—into a love affair of the noble and romantic category in which one no longer distinguishes between bodily and spiritual appetite or satiety!" (Dinesen, 1953/1988:38)

Everyone at Babette's table undergoes a transformation; Ba-bette's art is the medium. Voices long silent speak again; warm memories are retrieved; ascetics become convivial storytellers.

> Usually in Berlevaag people did not speak much while they were eating. But somehow this evening tongues had been loosened. An old Brother told the story of his first meeting with the Dean. Another went through that sermon which sixty years ago had brought about his conversion. An aged woman, the one to whom Martine had first confided her distress, reminded her friends how in all afflictions any Brother or Sister was ready to share the burden of any other. (Dinesen, 1953/1988:36)

It would be a pity to miss Isak Dinesen's inimitable description of her characters and what further transpires at Babette's com-munion table on this holy night:

> Of what happened later in the evening nothing definite can here be stated. None of the guests later on had any clear remembrance of it. They only knew that the rooms had been filled with a heavenly light, as if a number of small halos had blended into one glorious radiance. Taciturn old people received the gift of tongues; ears that for years had been almost deaf were opened to it. Time itself had merged into eternity. Long after midnight the windows of the house shone like gold, and golden song flowed out into the winter air. (Dinesen, 1953/1988:41)

Old grudges and fixations give way to "heavenly light," laughter, hope, and reconciliation:

The two old women who had once slandered each other now in their hearts went back a long way, past the evil period in which they had been stuck, to those days of their early girlhood when together they had been preparing for confirmation and hand in hand had filled the roads round Berlevaag with singing. A Brother in the congregation gave another a knock in the ribs, like a rough caress between boys, and cried out: 'You cheated me on that timber, you old scoundrel!' The Brother thus addressed almost collapsed in a heavenly burst of laughter, but tears ran from his eyes. 'Yes, I did so, beloved Brother,' he answered. 'I did so.' Skipper Halvorsen and Madam Oppegaarden suddenly found themselves close together in a corner and gave one another that long, long kiss, for which the secret uncertain love affair of their youth had never left them time. (Dinesen, 1953/1988:42)

The elderly brothers and sisters become like boys and girls again, poking one another in the ribs, laughing heartily in "heavenly" bursts, tears streaming from their eyes. Their stories are unstuck, picked up again, and a new start ensues for estranged friends long alienated from themselves and one another. General Loewenhielm is reconciled to his long-ago decision and the many years without Martine. They part again in peace.

Leaving the party, the guests bless one another and the new that has come for them all. In childlike frolic, their glee rings through the night, changing it to dawn. They themselves have been changed, and the reader knows that it will be lasting.

Finally, at the conclusion of the feast, Dinesen turns to its artist. Now the focus is on Babette. Martine and Philippa worry that Babette will return to Paris, and they approach her with their concern. She reassures them that she has no intention of leaving; she no longer has a life there.

"No," said Babette. "What will I do in Paris? They have all gone. I have lost them all, Mesdames."

The sisters' thoughts went to Monsieur Hersant and his son, and they said: "Oh, my poor Babette."

"Yes, they have all gone," said Babette. "The Duke of Morny, the Duke of Decazes, Prince Narishkine, General Galliffet, Aurélian Scholl, Paul Daru, the Princesse Pauline! All!" (Dinesen, 1953/1988:45)

The sisters learn that Babette, furthermore, has spent her entire ten thousand francs on the banquet. They are speechless at this revelation. It is here that Dinesen expresses a view of the nature of self-sacrifice with which Christians have had scant acquaintance, and it has to do only tangentially with the ten thousand francs. Dinesen explicitly names Babette's act an act of self-sacrifice.

Philippa, herself gifted with a great artistic talent, begins slowly to awaken to what she has witnessed on this revelatory evening. Assuming that Babette has spent all her money for their sakes only and unconsciously espousing an ancient dualism of self and other, Philippa at first protests:

> "Dear Babette," she said softly, "you ought not to have given away all you had for our sake."
>
> Babette gave her mistress a deep glance, a strange glance. Was there not pity, even scorn, at the bottom of it?
>
> "For your sake?" she replied. "No. For my own."
>
> She rose from the chopping block and stood up before the two sisters.
>
> "I am a great artist!" she said.
>
> She waited a moment and then repeated: "I am a great artist, Mesdames."
>
> Again for a long time there was deep silence in the kitchen.
>
> Then Martine said: "So you will be poor now all your life, Babette?"
>
> "Poor?" said Babette. She smiled as if to herself. "No, I shall never be poor. I told you that I am a great artist. A great artist, Mesdames, is never poor. We have something, Mesdames, of which other people know nothing." (Dinesen, 1953/1988:46, 47)

Now, Philippa begins to become aware of a profound and complex truth, one that she never came to know in her own experience because she had closed off its possibility:

> While the elder sister found nothing more to say, in Philippa's heart deep, forgotten chords vibrated. For she had heard, before now, long ago, of the Café Anglais. She had heard, before now, long ago, the names on Babette's tragic list. She rose and took a step toward her servant.
>
> "But all those people whom you have mentioned," she said, "those princes and great people of Paris whom you named, Babette? You yourself fought against them. You were a Communard! The General you named had your husband and son shot! How can you grieve over them?"
>
> Babette's dark eyes met Philippa's.

"Yes," she said, "I was a Communard. Thanks be to God, I was a Communard! And those people whom I named, Mesdames, were evil and cruel. They let the people of Paris starve; they oppressed and wronged the poor. Thanks be to God, I stood upon a barricade; I loaded the gun for my menfolk! But all the same Mesdames, I shall not go back to Paris, now that those people of whom I have spoken are no longer there."

She stood immovable, lost in thought.

"You see, Mesdames," she said, at last, "those people belonged to me, they were mine. They had been brought up and trained, with greater expense than you, my little ladies, could ever imagine or believe, to understand what a great artist I am. I could make them happy. When I did my very best I could make them perfectly happy. (Dinesen, 1953/1988:48)

At this point, Babette pauses and then moves closer to the tragic circumstances of Philippa's own story. She knows what Philippa had relinquished by her rejection of Achille Papin's love and his offer to train her inimitable voice for the delight of those same Parisians and her own deep gratification. For the first time in many years, Papin's name is spoken in the sisters' household:

"It was like that with Monsieur Papin too," she said.

"With Monsieur Papin?" Philippa asked.

"Yes, with your Monsieur Papin, my poor lady," said Babette. "He told me so himself: 'It is terrible and unbearable to an artist,' he said, 'to be encouraged to do, to be applauded for doing, his second best.' He said: 'Through all the world there goes one long cry from the heart of the artist: Give me leave to do my utmost!'" (Dinesen, 1953/1988:48)

Philippa sees now what she can no longer repress. What has been pressed down and denied will not stay down.

Philippa went up to Babette and put her arms round her. She felt the cook's body like a marble monument against her own, but she herself shook and trembled from head to foot.

For a while she could not speak. (Dinesen, 1953/1988:48)

Then, with the same words that Achille Papin had said to her so long ago, speaking more of herself than Babette, Philippa whispers:

"Yet this is not the end! I feel Babette, that this is not the end. In Paradise you will be the great artist that God meant you to be! Ah!"

31

she added, the tears streaming down her cheeks. "Ah, how you will enchant the angels!" (Dinesen, 1953/1988:48).

Philippa's tears are for herself. They are at one and the same time tears of loss and grief, and tears of hope and blessing. Philippa's dualisms have been dislodged through Babette's own refusal to respond to life dualistically.

In giving most fully to herself by expressing her genius redemptively, Babette has sacrificed herself to others. There is no room here for an either-or dualism which requires one to deny her own truest self for the sake of others. Quite to the contrary, Dinesen shows us the fallacy of that ubiquitous dichotomy. Philippa has withheld her gift from others and herself. Babette, on the other hand, has given hers even to her enemies. In so doing, she has transcended the friend/enemy barrier, as well as enjoyed the greatest personal happiness she can know. She has stated it clearly: being able to make others happy by "doing her utmost" is the quintessence of life itself. Babette can, without arrogance, claim her genius. She knows that she is a great artist and is able to say so confidently and without bombast. She had sacrificed nothing of herself in the way that Philippa had through deciding not to develop her great singing voice. Nor had Babette reserved her enormous talent for a few cloistered relatives and friends, as Philippa had chosen to do. Instead, she had cooked for the intelligentsia and powerful gentry of Paris, and in Berlevaag for the widows and orphans. Refusing to divide the world into dichotomous camps, Babette mourns the very people whom she and her husband and son resisted in the conflict. As she states, " ... those people belonged to me, they were mine. ... When I did my very best I could make them perfectly happy" (Dinesen, 1953/1988:48).

Paradoxically *Babette has sacrificed herself through a consummate act of self-affirmation.* By giving to herself most redemptively and genuinely, she has given herself sacrificially to others. Paraphrasing Bonhoeffer, I think we can say that Babette has not sinned at the point of her greatest strength. Dinesen leaves us wondering if Philippa has not. And therein lies Philippa's tragedy. Wishing to sacrifice herself to Christian service and to assist her father's ministry, she has withheld Philippa herself. *Sacrifice has become waste, not gift.*

Dinesen has, in this story, cast a new light on the Jesus Story. Interlacing the contemporary literary story and the normative biblical story, I have seen what at times has alarmed and angered me in Christian theology's reading of its central narrative. *We have failed to take note of Jesus' refusal to deny himself in our concentration on Jesus' denial of himself.* Can anyone challenge the assertion that Jesus expressed his genius, his gifts, fully? Choosing to be who he most truly was, Jesus refused to deny his genius, his greatest gifts, the fullness of the person he was. That is hardly self-denial. Or, it is hardly self-denial according to Philippa's terms or those to which we are most accustomed. But looked at from a full-orbed perspective, it was only so that Jesus could give himself most fully to others.

When I was a little girl growing up in eastern North Carolina, I learned that the church frowned heavily on "pride" and approved heartily of self-denial, which it understood as the opposite of pride. Pride seemed to be any thought given to the self and its needs and desires. Self-denial meant despising one's own aspirations and always "preferring others." We were taught in Sunday School to spell "sin" as "sIn", emphasizing the "I." Later, I came to realize that this simplistic view was not too far off the mark of the broader Christian tradition's perspective on the value of the self.

Babette's Feast (and a close reading of the gospels) fails to match this view, however. Dinesen shows us that true self-sacrifice and self-denial, paradoxically, focus not on weakness but on strength and are consistent with something which Dietrich Bonhoeffer recognizes in his letters from Tegel Military Prison. There, Bonhoeffer says that human beings sin most gravely at the point of their strengths, not their weaknesses (Bonhoeffer, 1953/1979). Bonhoeffer suggests that we might even be expected to sin at the point of our weaknesses; the idea is not to condone this reality but simply to acknowledge it. But sinning at the point of our strengths has more serious consequences not only for us personally but for others affected by our actions, as well. Either failing to express our particular strengths for the good of humankind and the creation, or, more perversely, expressing our gifts intentionally for destructive ends redounds to the injury of us all. We can think of examples. Hitler's charisma and military genius were strengths employed for demonic ends. Their destructive consequences were an injury to humanity beyond our capacity to imagine before that time. Conversely, Martin Luther King, Jr.'s strengths of vision and leadership directed toward human good continue to reap constructive benefits for white Americans as well as African Americans here and for others around the globe. King sacrificed his gifts and himself ultimately. But in so doing, he was and became most truly and fully himself. This was genuine self-denial on the model of Christ, a paradox of losing and gaining the self in one movement. It was in this sense that Jesus was, as Bonhoeffer declared him, a man for others.

Dinesen's use of religious allusion is ingredient to her story of christic self-denial. The reader needs to examine that usage carefully. Dinesen weaves religious references so skillfully and subtly into her story that their impact is made with the reader's only partial awareness of their presence and function. Let us return to the banqueters. Made convivial by the sacramental feast Babette has prepared, a Sister tells the story of the Dean's extraordinary ministry to them on a Christmas long ago:

> Did they remember, she asked, the time when he had promised a Christmas sermon in the village the other side of the fjord? For a fortnight the weather had been so bad that no skipper or fisherman would risk the crossing. The villagers were giving up hope, but the Dean told them that if no boat would take him, *he would come to them walking upon the waves.* And behold! Three days before Christmas the storms stopped, hard frost set in, and the fjord froze from shore to shore—and this was a thing which had not happened within the memory of man! (Dinesen, 1953/1988:36, 37, emphasis added)

Dinesen's Christological allusion in the elderly Sister's story takes its place within the grand story of grace that she is weaving. The rigid founder of this Lutheran sect had, at one and the same time, been one who had impeded his daughters' and parishioners' full enjoyment of and expression of God's grace, *and* one who had related to them as Christ. There had been times when he had "walked on the water," and those were no less real than the life-denying asceticism limiting their enjoyment of God's goodness. Dinesen thus demonstrates her refusal to divide up the world dualistically and draw any part of it or any individual in reductionistic and exclusivistic terms.

As the dinner progresses, one after another brother and sister becomes talkative and cordial, even sociable, and one after another listens eagerly to her or his table companion: "Taciturn old people *received the gift of tongues*; ears that for years had been almost deaf were opened to it" (Dinesen, 1953/1988:41). Dinesen's allusion is to the Pentecost passage in Acts in which the Spirit is poured out upon all those congregated and they are enabled to communicate with understanding. Here, too, at Babette's table, the Spirit has broken barriers and restored communication. Friendships are reclaimed and old grudges forgiven. It all has come through gift.

When these reconciled friends depart for their homes still playful with celebration, Dinesen employs religious allusion to describe the profound work of grace that has been wrought through Babette's gift of her genius:

> When at last the company broke up it had ceased to snow. The town and the mountains lay in white, unearthly splendor and the sky was bright with thousands of stars. In the street the snow was lying so deep that it had become difficult to walk. The guests from the yellow house wavered on their feet, staggered, sat down abruptly or fell forward on their knees and hands and were covered with snow, *as if they had indeed had their sins washed white as wool*, and in this regained innocent attire were gamboling like little lambs. It was, to each of them, blissful *to have become as a small child*; it was also a blessed joke to watch old Brothers and Sisters, who had been taking themselves so seriously, in this kind of celestial second childhood. They stumbled and got up, walked on or stood still, bodily as well as spiritually hand in hand, at moments performing the great chain of a beatified *lanciers*.
>
> "Bless you, bless you, bless you," like an echo of the harmony of the spheres rang on all sides. (Dinesen, 1953/1988 43:, emphasis added)

With the giving and accepting of forgiveness, they have been cleansed of their sins and have become like children, trusting, playful, and jubilant. Jesus' admonition to become like children comes to mind, as does his description of the effect of forgiveness.

Much more subtle is Dinesen's allusion in the final scene to Babette's servanthood and its christic role in the transformation which all in the fellowship have experienced this sacred night. Babette has been Martine's and Philippa's cook, housekeeper, and "French maid-of-all-work." But now, for the first time, Dinesen refers to her as their *servant*. With characteristic and exquisite terseness, Dinesen writes concerning Philippa: "She rose and took a step toward her servant" (Dinesen, 1953/1988:47). We are reminded of another brief Dinesenian statement: "She can cook." As with that earlier understatement, we might miss the significance of this deceptively simple assertion were it not for other statements which Dinesen makes preparing her readers for a final Christological allusion so subtle as almost to be a throw-away. Six paragraphs into her story, Dinesen states that Babette's presence in the Dean's household cannot be accounted for solely by the fact that the sisters receive her as a "friendless fugitive," but that the "true reason for Babette's presence in the two sisters' house was to be found further back in time and deeper down in the domain of human hearts." Thereby, Dinesen early on suggestively points her readers toward Babette's redemptive, christic role. Later, the Christological allusion cannot be missed:

> In the course of time not a few of the brotherhood included Babette's name in their prayers, and thanked God for the speechless stranger, the dark Martha in the house of their two fair Marys. *The stone which the builders had almost refused had become the headstone of the corner.* (Dinesen, 1953/1988:17, emphasis added)

With this backdrop as preparation, Dinesen names Babette at the end of the narrative as "her servant." By now, the reader has witnessed all that Dinesen, the consummate storyteller, has earlier foreshadowed. The religious significance of Babette's ministrations has been richly validated. No one is the same, including Babette.

We need here to reflect theologically, with care, on the story of transforming grace which Dinesen is developing. The fact that grace as she perceives and describes it through the characters, plot, and setting of her story is Christological grace should not escape us. Though she nowhere says so explicitly, Dinesen weaves an intricate, subtle, and powerful story of grace mediated through Christ and the story of Christ. This fact seems incontrovertible when we look closely at the religious allusions she has selected and incorporated, using them to fund her narrative with meaning apart from which her masterpiece would be, at most, an interesting story useful for the reader's diversion and enjoyment. The biblical allusions she includes are to the story of Jesus' walking on the water, his identity as cornerstone of the church and of the commonwealth of God, his work of self-expending servanthood, the consequent transformation of sinners as those washed white as wool and reconciled and renewed as small children, and the pentecostal miracle of restored communication as brother to brother and sister to sister, each to all alike. By employing these biblical elements, Dinesen interprets and identifies her literary creation as a story of Christological grace.

Babette's culinary genius has functioned as a channel for that grace. Through the senses of taste, smell, sight, and texture, a sacramental, reconciling work has been wrought. Love has been shed through food and drink, non-sensate elements natural and fashioned. A "walking on the water" has occurred again; a celebration of the miraculous nature of the creation itself is contained in Isak Dinesen's sacramental view of organic things. Herein, Dinesen expresses her view that the heartbeat of the world is aesthetic, playful, and mystical, rather than moral. She might even be saying something like what many psychologists say: that one cannot be good without first being happy. This view has nothing to do with hedonism; it is about delight, joy, celebration, play, and creativity. In Dinesen's estimation, we might say this little band of Lutherans (and, by implication, we all) have lost the "joy of our salvation." Life is less moral than mystical, set to the music of the spheres as the ancients knew but then forgot, Dinesen seems to be saying.

Dinesen's perspective has kinship with much else that is old in Christian theology and also much that is relatively new. The processive nature of becoming and salvation, akin to Irenaeus's second century insight and also to that of twentieth-century process thinkers influenced in part themselves by Irenaeus, is a view analogous to Dinesen's. The elderly Brothers and Sisters of Berlevaag had been shut down, in significant respects, in their growth toward full Christian personhood and maturity. However, narrative insights need to be inserted here to correct any suggestion that Dinesen's characters' development is mechanistic rather than story-shaped. Rather, Babette's gift to them orients them again in the Christian story and creates room for the work of divine grace.

Although the Christological nature of grace is primarily conveyed through religious allusion, Dinesen is nonetheless other-

37

wise explicit; she has much to say about grace. *Babette's Feast* is about grace. Embodied grace. Grace through art and life and gift. Indeed, Dinesen at last forsakes her unequaled art of understatement and suggestion lest her readers miss the point. General Loewenhielm's speech is evidently Dinesen's own meditation on grace:

> "Mercy and truth, my friends, have met together," said the General. "Righteousness and bliss shall kiss one another." . . .
>
> "Man, my friends, "said General Loewenhielm," is frail and foolish. We have all of us been told that grace is to be found in the universe. But in our human foolishness and short-sightedness we imagine divine grace to be finite. For this reason we tremble . . . " Never till now had the General stated that he trembled; he was genuinely surprised and even shocked at hearing his own voice proclaim the fact. "We tremble before making our choice in life, and after having made it again tremble in fear of having chosen wrong. But the moment comes when our eyes are opened, and we see and realize that grace is infinite. Grace, my friends, demands nothing from us but that we shall await it with confidence and acknowledge it in gratitude. Grace, brothers, makes no conditions and singles out none of us in particular; grace takes us all to its bosom and proclaims general amnesty. See! that which we have chosen is given us, and that which we have refused is, also and at the same time, granted us. Ay, that which we have rejected is poured upon us abundantly. For mercy and truth have met together and righteousness and bliss have kissed one another! (Dinesen, 1953/1988:39-41)

Years ago, the young Lieutenant Loewenhielm had been speechless at the Dean's dinner table. On this night, he has been granted even that which he had refused; his voice rings eloquently and truly.

The Christological, sacramental grace shed by Dinesen's story *itself* is overwhelming. It transforms us by transforming our insights. *Babette's Feast* shows that God's grace is, indeed, unlimited. Despite the limitations of the Dean and his sect, grace has still been mediated through them. Again, Dinesen rejects a dualistic either-or perspective. Grace has been present in Berlevaag: following the example and commission of Jesus, this small band of Lutheran Christians has lived the Jesus Story faithfully enough that the poor have been fed, the homeless housed, the sick attended; there have been countless "smaller miracles of kindliness and helpfulness daily performed." Dinesen's story is not, in the final analysis, the story of lost gifts but of grace permeating, suffusing, all that is. It is the story of Jacob struggling with the angel, demanding the blessing and getting it. And the Jacob story is Isak Dinesen's model for her own personal life story.

Finally, *Babette's Feast* is about the sacredness and blessing of story. General Loewenhielm at last is able to bless his own story. Babette blesses her story: those who had dined on her superlative cuisine at Café Anglais had killed her husband and son. Still, those same people were hers. The entire story is hers, and it is sacred. Philippa, too, is able to bless her story. Her tears are tears of loss and grief, but also tears of thanksgiving and hope. Dinesen's embrace of story with her refusal to centrifuge pain from joy and death from resurrection comes out of her own experience, her struggle with the angel. Like Jacob, she emerges halt but blessed. We shall look at this further in part II in our analysis of stories of "the human heart in conflict with itself."

Now, however, it is time to look directly at the biblical narratives and to interlace those with the contemporary narratives which we have investigated and particularly with *Babette's Feast*.

Interlacing Biblical and Contemporary Narratives

The narrative method which I am offering here is a methodology which is both *reproductive* and *productive* in its task. Ancient insights belonging to the Christian community are *reproduced* again, and insights newly born are *produced*, attesting to the scripture's liveliness, its nature as a "living word" of God. Hence, I am offering in these pages an interpretation of Jesus' self-sacrifice and role as a "man for others" which is reproductive in some aspects and thereby familiar, but productive in other aspects and largely unfamiliar.

I believe it is important to begin with the story of the boy in the temple. We have read this narrative in Luke and wondered at Jesus' precocity, marveled at his lack of fear at being left behind, worried with Mary and Joseph as they searched for him, felt a little put out by his seeming insensitivity to his mother's distress, and finally been generally pleased to have this early picture of the boy Jesus whom we later come to know as teacher of the teachers themselves. I appreciate the New Revised Standard Version's translation of the exchange between Jesus and his mother. It shows that Mary peevishly tries to evoke her son's guilt for putting her through so much worry, "Child, why have you treated us like this? Look, your father and I have been searching for you in great anxiety." Jesus' reply shows that it has not worked. He does not feel guilty. Instead, he suggests that she should have expected him to be exactly where he was. "Why were you searching for me? Did you not know that I must be in my Father's house?" (Luke 2:48, 49).

Luke has given us here a portrait of a precocious and self-aware child, comfortable with his own growing powers and able to stretch them and enjoy them. Though Jesus returns to Nazareth with his parents and continues to be "obedient to them," he is not afflicted with the notion that he has been disobedient and bad and should have forfeited his valuable time with the teachers in order to have spared his parents their anxiety. Luke has allowed us to see here, developing in Jesus, an uncommon understanding of what giving himself means. This growing self-knowledge will continue to emerge in ways which shatter our expectations, even as Jesus' behavior as a pre-pubescent youth does in this narrative.

There will be, however, a red thread running consistently through all the stories depicting who Jesus is and how he understands his self-giving. We encounter it first here in his response to Mary's exasperated and anxious question: "Did you not know that I must be in my Father's house?" Luke foreshadows what will come. *In Jesus' view, self-giving, self-denial, self-sacrifice will be understood always in terms of what it means to be in God's house.* This is the red thread connecting all parts of the fabric of his story. Self-sacrifice according to the world's perspective, the synagogue's, or his mother's, will not be Jesus' rule for shaping his behavior and ministry. He will make uncommon choices, therefore, and he will take uncommon actions. These, furthermore, as the temple story predicts, will be choices and actions *intimately connected to Jesus' own particular and peculiar genius.* Just as Jesus' early identity and powers have not been connected to driving camels on the journey home or constructing tables in Joseph's carpentry shop, but rather in "sitting among the teachers, listening to them and asking them questions" and amazing the teachers with "his understanding and his answers," Jesus' later decisions and actions will

40

conform to the self he most richly and profoundly is, even as they do at this early stage. Precisely by matching thought, decision, and deed to gift, genius, and art, Jesus becomes the man for others, the one who lives most truly and redemptively in God's house. *Self-sacrifice as Jesus models it defies our expectations.* We are accustomed to expecting something more like withdrawal and passivity, or at least self-demurral. What we get, time after time in the gospel stories, however, is self-assertion, self-confidence, confounding self-presentation bordering on arrogance! Is it not outright sassy and presumptuous of a twelve-year-old Jesus to answer his worried mother the way he does? Such thoughts will continue to surprise us as we follow Jesus' journey.

Self-sacrifice is never a value in and of itself for Jesus. It is never a divine principle to be followed. *Self-sacrifice has meaning only in relation to dwelling in the house of God.* It will be helpful to take some time for looking at what the Bible tells us about God's house. Then, we will be enabled to understand how Jesus' decisions and actions dovetail with what it means for him to live in that house and thereby to live self-sacrificially.

The gospel stories tell us that God's house is spacious with many rooms prepared, furthermore, for inhabitants like us (John 14:2). It is one in which siblings living together may or may not be blood kin (Mark 3:35). What is most important is their wish and intention to dwell with one another in God's house. God's house is one in which feasts are planned and given and to which people of all stations are invited (Matthew 22:10). Abundant, celebrative life characterizes the kind of living offered in God's house. Its inhabitants are peace-loving and peacemaking people (Matthew 5:9). The weary and burdened find respite there (Matthew 11:28–30). While the house has rooms, it has no barriers. The poor, the sick, the despised, outcast, unvalued, hungry and thirsty, the stranger, *all* find dwelling there (Matthew 25:34–36). Joyous, free, true, and abundant life characterizes the house's owner and its inhabitants. Jubilant life is life in God's house.

Living in God's house means living in the kingdom of God. The older metaphor has currency still, but the metaphor of life in the household of God has been convincingly employed and developed by Letty Russell and others and seems to me closer to the Bible, even, than the kingdom metaphor. (Russell, 1987; 1993). Multiple images of God's house in the gospels have been, until recent years, by and large overlooked in favor of kingdom imagery. Household imagery, however, evokes appreciation for the intent and content of God's relations with humankind and all creation as metaphorically those of family relations, characterized by love, nurture, hospitality toward neighbor and stranger alike, encouragement, and enablement toward maturity. For those reasons, I have elected to develop the image and theme of God's house rather than of God's kingdom.

Let us turn, now, to the narrative of Jesus, the young man on the brink of his ministry and its inauguration, recorded in Luke. Will we recognize the boy we saw in the temple in Jerusalem? I think so. Again, Luke shows us a startlingly confident Jesus, assertive, sure of himself, compellingly attractive when he speaks, obviously in his element. Designated the reader in his hometown synagogue on this auspicious sabbath, Jesus reads the passage from Isaiah selected for this day. Luke cracks the door of the synagogue and allows the reader-hearer to glimpse the congregation, hear Jesus' address, and witness his effect on the hometown folk. They are transfixed, mesmerized by the grace and beauty of his reading. The familiar words have never sounded so powerful and true, so convincing and attractive. They whisper among themselves, breathless with what they are seeing and hearing: "Is not this Joseph's son?" But the beauty of his words and the strength of Jesus' presence are not all that Luke shows us. Echoes of the twelve-year-old's reply to his mother are heard in Jesus' assertion after he has taken his seat. "Today this scripture has been fulfilled in your hearing." As if that were not enough for these folk to absorb, he puts words into their mouths, answering their objections before they make them: "Doubtless you will quote to me this proverb, 'Doctor, cure yourself!' And you will say, 'Do here also in your hometown the things that we have heard you did at Capernaum" (Luke 4:23).

We can only guess why he taunts these hometown folk who know him as Joseph's boy with stories of faithlessness in Elijah's and Elisha's time, implying that they, also, are lacking in faith. Perhaps he is a little unsure of himself, after all, despite this enormous claim to be the fulfillment of Isaiah's prophetic, messianic vision. And we can understand why some of his supreme self-confidence might be bravado on the part of a young man just starting out on an overwhelming mission. If he overstates his case in order to quell his own misgivings and finds himself in trouble thereby, perhaps that is not so surprising. In any case, we know he is going to follow through on the course he has described for himself. Just as he stayed behind in the temple as a boy to learn all that he could, now he will stay to his course to be all that he knows he is. His methodology might be a little rough at the edges, but his self-knowledge is on target; he knows what his genius is. Like Babette, he can say with conviction, "I am a great artist."

Jesus' art is exactly what he has, with Isaiah's words, just described for these Nazarenes. He is the fulfillment of the messianic promise. He is not *just* Joseph the carpenter's son. He has been gifted with a supreme gift, a great genius, a consummate talent, and like that of all great artists, his genius will be known in its expression. His self-giving, his self-sacrifice, like Babette's, will be the full living out of his splendid talent. Jesus' gift, furthermore, is directly related to life in God's house. Because of him, his proclamation of liberation, his Spirit-anointing and ministry, others' lives will be transformed. Both the great burden and unparalleled joy of a unique journey now lie spread out before him. Because of him, the poor will hear good news, captives will be released, the sightless will see, the oppressed will stand free, all will experience the Lord's favor.

Let us proceed to the calling of the disciples. To live in God's house, both eternally and historically, beyond history and within it, and to open the doors for others to do the same, Jesus knows, will require a community of inhabitants dedicated to his vision. Stalwart and energetic though he be, he cannot carry it off by himself. The evangelists give us scant pictures, at best, of Jesus' enlistment of his disciples. We might wish that they had dwelt longer on this important phase of Jesus' preparation for the long road ahead. Trying to understand the appeal that convinced this diverse band of people to drop everything they were doing to sign up with Jesus the Nazarene requires us to backtrack and look again at what we already have observed about Jesus' unique charisma. Already possessing uncommon attributes at the age of twelve, such that the unimpressionable doctors and teachers in the Jerusalem temple took notice—"All who heard him *were amazed* at his understanding and his answers"—Jesus has a history of affecting people in unexpected ways. The same phenomenon occurred in the synagogue at Nazareth, as we have seen:

43

"The eyes of all in the synagogue were fixed on him . . . All spoke well of him and *were amazed* at the gracious words that came from his mouth" (emphasis added). Twice Jesus' effect on others has been described as amazement. Although the gospel narratives do not explicitly report the same kind of "answers" and "gracious words" spoken to the disciples by Jesus as he draws them to join him, I think we are justified in assuming that Simon and Andrew, James and John, and their cohorts, were persuaded by the same uncommon personality that had amazed others for most of Jesus' life. They sign up with alacrity, it seems. And never do we see them seriously considering going back home again.

What has interested me most about the calling of the disciples, however, is the disparity between the usual interpretation of Jesus as one who never, or seldom, thought of himself, which I have heard either explicitly or tacitly most of my life, and what actually stands out here. Is it true that Jesus is self-effacing and other-regarding at his own expense? Or is he able to regard others respectfully in proportion to his genuine and true self regard? What kind of interaction occurs between Jesus and these persons? Are Jesus' words and manner self-deprecatory?

> And Jesus said to them, "Follow me, and I will make you fish for people!"And immediately they left their nets and followed him. (Mark 1:17)

What kind of man feels justified in calling other men (and women?) away from their occupations and life plans to become those who learn from him and advance his vision? It seems strange to me that we have tagged Jesus as self-effacing and self-negating. Out of the strength of a high and composed self regard directed toward God's own intentions for humankind and the world, Jesus, in the language of the Christian tradition, in-augurates the kingdom of God. Said differently, Jesus indwells God's house and draws others into that same sacred household. Jesus knows his own great worth, is thankful for it and knows its divine source, and is able to value all others as of great worth, as well. Performing what on the face of it appears to be an audacious, even arrogant, act (as also in the Jerusalem temple and the Naz-areth synagogue), Jesus opens out uncommon potentialities of heretofore very ordinary personalities. Each of these people be-comes more than he or she would otherwise have been. Their best

44

talents are unleashed by Jesus' unabashed expression of his own magnificent genius and art.

Dinesen's story has shown us something of the nature of this phenomenon. Babette's unfettered expression of her great art releases the guests around her banquet table for their own strongest, truest selves. Thus freed, they are enabled to become genuine community again, sparkling personalities blessing and supporting, appreciating and delighting in their neighbors. Jesus' calling of the disciples is our model par excellence for redemptive human relating, strength added to strength, power evoking power, all flowering to their fullest and truest for life in God's world (and otherworld) house. Nothing in this model supports the Enlightenment notion of unchecked self-interest. Jesus' (like Babette's) self regard is identical to profound self-sacrifice. The best of the self is poured out in a joyous, ecstatic dance of supernal artistry which can be appreciated fully only as a gift to self and others which is, on its truest level, praise of God the Gift-giver. No one is violated, unvalued, or undervalued, not the self nor the other. God is glorified and God's house is peopled. The weak, handicapped, retarded, aged, despised, the sinner, even the enemy, *all* are drawn into God's house where rooms have been prepared for them, even by Jesus the Christ.

Having called his disciples, Jesus' narrative continues. He now teaches, heals, feeds, liberates, redeems the people. We can expect his teaching to be spun by the red thread of hospitality identified early in the gospel story: *all that Jesus thinks, decides, and does points toward life in God's house and God's divine hospitality.* So what would we expect him to teach? What *does* he teach? Whatever we expected, somehow we are not prepared for what we get:

> Blessed are you who are poor,
>   for yours is the kingdom of God
> Blessed are you who are hungry now,
>   for you will be filled.
> Blessed are you who weep now,
>   for you will laugh.
> Blessed are you when people hate you, and when they exclude you, revile you, and defame you on account of the Son of Man (Luke 6:20–22).

The blessed, happy ones, or those who can expect to be happy, are the poor, the hungry, the weeping and hated ones, the excluded ones? How can that be so? At other places, Jesus suggests that rejected Samaritans, despised tax collectors, harlots and other unsavory characters, repulsive lepers and other untouchables, share this same hopeful expectation. Can it be that even God somehow identifies with, shares the same identity as, these lowly ones? Matthew's story of the final judgment makes a strong statement in support of such an incredible identification. Jesus' announcement in the synagogue at Nazareth earlier foreshadowed the same.

> When the Son of Man comes in his glory, and all the angels with him, then he will sit on the throne of his glory. All the nations will be gathered before him, and he will separate people one from another as a shepherd separates the sheep from the goats, and he will put the sheep at his right hand and the goats at the left. Then the king will say to those at his right hand, "Come, you that are blessed by my Father, inherit the kingdom prepared for you from the foundation of the world; for I was hungry and you gave me food, I was thirsty and you gave me something to drink, I was a stranger and you welcomed me, I was naked and you gave me clothing, I was sick and you took care of me, I was in prison and you visited me." Then the righteous will answer him, "Lord, when was it that we saw you a stranger and welcomed you, or naked and gave you clothing? And when was it that we saw you sick or in prison and visited you?" And the king will answer them, "Truly I tell you, just as you did it to one of the least of these who are members of my family, you did it to me. (Matthew 25:31–40)

The New Revised Standard Version's inclusion of the phrase *who are members of my family* emphasizes the familial identity of God and the lowly and suffering. Members of the same family, God and the lowly inhabit the same house. And those who have fed, clothed, and welcomed the suffering ones also are a part of that family, sharing God's house here and in the world to come.

All Jesus has said strikes the reader/hearer's ear, sending shock waves reverberating through the psyche. The happy ones are the suffering ones because they are members of God's own family! The happy ones are also those who take risks to alleviate the hunger, thirst, loneliness, and pain of others; they, too, are members of God's own family!

What he teaches Jesus also performs. Let us turn to the story of Jesus' feeding the multitudes. The hour is late; many have sat and listened to his teaching, we can surmise, not just patiently but enthralled. Now, they are hungry. Jesus' disciples approach him and suggest that he dismiss the people so that they may go into the village and get something to eat. But Jesus directs the disciples to feed them themselves. Startled by such an outlandish suggestion (they also have very little food) and probably somewhat worried that Jesus is requiring them to expend what little money they have on these people, they ask how this is feasible. Jesus tells them to get together the food they have (five loaves of bread and two fish, it turns out to be) and to assemble the people in groups. From here on, the story gets strange beyond anything we could have predicted.

> Taking the five loaves and the two fish, he looked up to heaven, and blessed and broke the loaves, and gave them to the disciples, and the disciples gave them to the crowds. And all ate and were filled; and they took up what was left over of the broken pieces, twelve baskets full. And those who ate were about five thousand men, besides women and children. (Matthew 14:19–21)

What happened here? Were the loaves and fish miraculously multiplied enough to feed thousands of people? Did the people *feel* satisfied despite the little food because of Jesus' blessing of it? I do not think we can do more than speculate. But what I would like to do is to interlace this story with Babette's story. While there are significant, even stark, differences, there are important similarities as well. The productive event emerging from the interlacing of the biblical story and Dinesen's narrative will, I believe, be one which evokes new insight for us.

Dinesen, as we have seen, draws Babette as a Christlike figure. Evocative religious allusion names her as "the cornerstone" nearly overlooked, and her feast is described as a heavenly meal. She is a person of genius, a great artist, who through her art transforms common elements of food and drink into an inimitable feast. Finally allowing themselves to enjoy this wonderful gift, the guests at Babette's table are themselves transformed. They become again, nay, they become for the first time, a true community of brothers and sisters, delighting in one another, forgiving, embracing, restoring, blessing one another, and delighting in the cuisine, the wine, and the banks of snow which they gambol and

47

stumble through as they depart. The whole world has become new for them.

Jesus is the Christ whom Babette is like. *He* is the cornerstone nearly overlooked, serving as the model for Dinesen as she draws Babette. Jesus is a person of genius, an incomparable artist, who transforms through his art the common elements of bread and fish into a heavenly meal satisfying the hunger of multitudes. But it is not the meal itself which serves as the medium of transformation in the biblical story, as it is in Dinesen's narrative. While Babette remains in the background and her banquet itself is at center stage, (at no point does she address the banqueters), in the biblical narrative the loaves and fish remain simple, plain fare and are never the focus of the story. It is Jesus himself who is the source of transformation. Jesus' artistry is more than what he does; it is what he is. Art and artist are one. They are identical. Only so could Jesus say to the hometown folk on that sabbath in Nazareth, "Today this scripture has been fulfilled in your hearing." The scripture had referred to a person; it had stressed first person objective: "The Spirit of the Lord is upon *me*, because he has anointed *me* to bring good news to the poor. He has sent *me* to proclaim release to the captives and recovery of sight to the blind . . . " The multitudes are filled because Jesus himself has been their food, their transforming gift.

Interlacing the two narratives yields what Hans-Georg Gadamer has referred to as a "third event." (Gadamer, 1976). Something is revealed about the nature of self-sacrifice, Babette's and Jesus'. Neither Babette nor Jesus sacrificed themselves by downplaying their outstanding gifts. Rather, exactly by expressing those astounding gifts with abandon, they sacrificed themselves truly and fully. Others were changed, blessed, thereby. There are implications for us all in this, and some long-standing ideas are challenged. Notions that self-sacrifice involves restraining oneself, pushing others out there in front of the footlights and remaining in the wings, are upset by both these stories. Jesus pushed his disciples out there, "Feed them yourselves," and *stepped out there with them*. Babette cooked as only she could and served a feast the likes of which only the General had ever seen before. We have to wonder how much has been lost to the human family and God's world house because the educationally and socially disadvantaged, the poor, women, those of dark skin, and others have been told that a proper humility meant standing in the background supporting others before the footlights. More than that, we have to wonder how God's house might now be peopled if we had read and told the Story aright for all these years. In God's house, self-expression and self-sacrifice have to do with the reality of Incarnation and continuing incarnation. We need to reflect on this for a moment.

How does self-sacrifice, that of Jesus and Babette, interlock paradoxically with self-expression, and how does that paradox tell us more about the mystery of the Incarnation? What does the paradox illumine concerning the primary Incarnation in Jesus and continuing incarnation in men and women like Babette and us? First of all, the notion I am setting forth here is not the Enlightenment exaltation of the individual; indeed, it has far more to do with community than atomistic individualism. Second, self-sacrifice *through* self-expression occurs concretely in narrative journeying through plot, character, and setting. Incarnation, en-fleshment, apart from character holds no meaning. The identifying gifts of any character, Jesus, Babette, or us, are the primary focus of personhood for that character and the primary seat of incarnation. Specifically at the point of identifying gift, the Gift-giver who is God is expressed in the character who embodies and enfleshes the identifying characteristic. Hence, exactly in the full, sacrificial expression of that gift which most identifies Babette as the specific person she is resides her part in the continuing incarnation. Jesus is himself the supreme Incarnation of God the Gift-giver in the full living out of his redemptive personhood. By living the full genius of who he is sacrificially, Jesus expresses and glorifies God.

All that which character embodies, enfleshes, and incarnates, occurs in eventful plot and concrete setting. Both Jesus' and Babette's sacrificial self-expression happen in specific events and particular places in which God's purposes of transformation and reconciliation are enacted. In specific events of worship, healing, feeding, preaching, teaching, and finally dying, Jesus expresses his gifts fully, sacrificially; and these particular events occur in locatable places—Nazareth, Galilee, Samaria, Jerusalem. In the particular event of preparing her inimitable feast and serving it, Babette enacts her own role in the divine-human work of reconciliation and transformation, and it is done in the specific place

49

of the yellow house in Berlevaag. The paradox of self-sacrificial self-expression has to do, at its heart, with narrative incarnation. This incarnation of God in reconciling, transforming narrative journeying through character, plot, and setting has always to do with self-sacrificial expending of identifying gift through acts of self-expression, glorifying, reflecting truly, the Giver of gifts and expanding the household of reconciliation and transformation known traditionally as God's kingdom. Let us add an important further link.

I have introduced biblical story and literary story and interlaced them, or more accurately, I have shown how their interlacing yields a third event of productive, as well as reproductive, interpretation, evoking insights not formerly seen so clearly. There is, however, a link in this chain of interpretation and understanding still missing, and it is one so important as to be the generative context within which this phenomenon occurs. *That link, that context, is worship and discipleship, the faith community's story of living the Christian Story as its own.* As George Lindbeck has clearly shown us, Christians are men, women, boys, and girls who have learned the stories of Israel, Jesus, and the church well enough that now they interpret their own lives and the world itself in terms of those stories. Christians learn these formative stories within the context of worshiping, nurturing community as those who have been baptized into the Story and who now dine at the Lord's Table, breaking bread with other sisters and brothers and drinking from the Lord's Cup with them. Within that lively and rich context of fellowship, the story of Jesus is re-enacted and refracted through the stories of baptized, communicant brothers and sisters like Mel Williams.

At Watts Street Baptist Church in Durham, North Carolina, Mel's rich gifts of preaching and singing and pastoring and drawing out the talents of others in the congregation are expressed in a manner which is at once celebrative, challenging, admonishing, nurturing, gleeful, and profound. Mel is an artist, musically and theologically, liturgically and linguistically. Every Sunday, Mel pours it all out. There is for him no standing in false humility in the shadows away from the footlights. Mel gives his best; with Babette he could very well say, "I am a great artist." Mel sacrifices himself truly, unstintingly, sabbath upon sabbath, for the sheep of his flock. He does so day after day, as well, in hospital rooms, beside new graves, and over more cups of coffee than are good for him. He does so leading the songs of peace marchers, coordinating the social ministries of his and other Durham churches, and peeling potatoes in soup kitchens. Mel is an artist. He models self-sacrifice every day.

Nannie Mae Herndon is another self-sacrificing artist in the Watts Street Baptist congregation. Nannie Mae is a retired fourth-grade teacher, a poet, and since 1988, a sufferer of myasthenia gravis. Has she slumped into the shadows, ever? When Nannie Mae learned that she had this dread disease, and after her doctors had, trying one medication after another, stabilized her symptoms, she set about organizing something Durham did not yet have, a chapter of myasthenia gravis sufferers and supporters, educating the public about this disease, raising funds to finance research for its eradication, and lending hope and community to its sufferers and their families and friends. Nannie Mae was instrumental in organizing the chapter and, only minimally slowed by her cane, has given it dynamic leadership. Her self-sacrifice is identical to full and extravagant expression of her gifts, pouring them out for the good of herself and others, enacting exactly what she loves most and does best.

Mel and Nannie Mae are two of many baptized, table companions at the Lord's Supper each first Sunday at Watts Street Baptist. In that believing community they read, hear, tell, learn, and live the Jesus Story, partially to be sure, stumblingly no doubt, but also truly. Through worship and discipleship, Mel and Nannie Mae continue the incarnation. They receive the sacrifices of one another with grateful hearts and give back their own. Together, they indwell God's world house and invite the stranger outside the gate to do the same.

Biblical story, literary story, biographical story, church story. These and many other narratives interlace to reveal who Jesus Christ is for us today. Knowing that, or at least *something* of who Jesus is for us today, we can then know who we are for one another, for the creation itself, and within God's intentions. Our place in God's house, and role to be filled, begin to come clear. Christology and anthropology link hands within the community of baptized believers at the Lord's Table.

Let us continue following Jesus' narrative. We have seen him learning from the teachers in the temple, announcing his ministry, calling his disciples, teaching them and others, and feeding the hungry. Jesus also pronounced judgment, and not in a milquetoast fashion. The pharisees and lawyers, to their consternation, are those singled out for the Galilean's judgment. They had expected it to be prostitutes, tax collectors, and other breakers of the five points of rabbinic law. But they learn that Jesus has another rule or standard of measurement for evaluating actions. I think we know what it is by now. Again, the red thread shines for us to follow its trail. *What attitudes and actions are consistent with those of inhabitants of God's house? This is Jesus' yardstick.* Which convictions and practices open the door to God's house and fill it with grace, compassion, peace, justice, and love?

> "Woe to you Pharisees! For you tithe mint and rue and herbs of all kinds, and neglect justice and the love of God; it is these you ought to have practiced, without neglecting the others . . . Woe also to you lawyers! For you load people with burdens hard to bear, and you yourselves do not lift a finger to ease them. Woe to you! For you build the tombs of the prophets whom your ancestors killed. . . . Woe to you lawyers! For you have taken away the key of knowledge; you did not enter yourselves, and you have hindered those who were entering." (Luke 11:42,46,47,52)

Jesus is never interested in knowledge merely for the sake of knowing. The entrance which the lawyers have themselves failed to make and hindered others' making is an entrance into knowledge functioning as key to God's world house. Preferring seats of honor in the synagogue and maintenance of the prophets' tombs to entry into God's house, the pharisees and lawyers have fashioned their own judgment.

Can we discern the boy in the temple and the brand-new minister at the synagogue in the seasoned declaimer calling the powerful to accountability? Yes, again Jesus is confident, sure of his mission and his gifts for filling it. I think we can hear his voice ringing through the house. He is doing what he is best at and, though we might imagine that calling the self-righteous to repentance is less pleasant for him than feeding the hungry multitudes and healing the sick, Jesus is never more strongly himself than now. And here we begin to be uneasily aware that Jesus' self-sacrifice will lead ultimately to death itself. Being most truthfully who he is, Jesus challenges the mighty, those who have power to execute him. Is he oblivious to that fact? Does he know what he is risking? Jesus knows. And he also knows that he is at this very moment doing what in all the world he wants most to do, being most truly who he is, living his story most faithfully. I can imagine that the adrenaline is flowing like a geyser; Jesus' face is flushed, his breath quick and shallow, and his eyes flashing with vigor and courage. He is trembling, more than slightly. For this very hour he was born and for it, yes, he will die. His self-sacrifice is at this moment placed squarely on the altar. Every nuance of his un-matched personality, his consummate artistry, and invincible skill and resolve is in this moment expressed. Nothing is held back. He is at his strongest. This moment is his most fulfilling. Why? Because the challenge to his ministry is greatest here, and his words of judgment are both a call to repentance and an invitation to enter and indwell the house of God. Like Babette, he has spent his ten thousand francs. Like Nannie Mae, he has risen from the bed of myasthenia gravis to raise others from theirs. And recipro-cally, Babette and Nannie Mae, like him, have spent it all, their personal all, their art and genius. He is their cornerstone. Will those whom Jesus is now exhorting respond? Will he also be their cornerstone?

Jesus' gift-giving of his own person as cornerstone of God's house involves also a surprising capacity for receiving from oth-ers what he needs. We can look at the familiar story of the hemorrhaging woman for an amazing example of this reciprocal giving and receiving of gifts. Teaching, feeding, judging, Jesus heals both body and soul, both physical hurt and psychic despair. Others act, at the same time, as gift-givers to him. I have for many years, perhaps because I am a woman, empathized with the suffering woman in Luke 8. She is such a gift-giver to Jesus. Her story is an enlightening contrast to the story of the self-sufficient lawyers and Pharisees:

> Now there was a woman who had been suffering from hemor-
> rhages for twelve years; and though she had spent all she had on
> physicians, no one could cure her. She came up behind him and
> touched the fringe of his clothes, and immediately her hemorrhage
> stopped. Then Jesus asked, "Who touched me?" When all denied
> it, Peter said, "Master, the crowds surround you and press in on
> you." But Jesus said, "Someone touched me; for I noticed that
> power had gone out from me." When the woman saw that she

could not remain hidden, she came trembling; and falling down before them, she declared in the presence of all the people that she had touched him, and how she had been immediately healed. He said to her, "Daughter, your faith has made you well; go in peace." (Luke 8:43–48)

This is a fascinating story, brief but packed with movement, feeling, and drama. Like most of the stories within the Jesus narrative, this one has surprising elements whose full impact could miss us, in part because we are so totally caught off guard. How do we account for Luke's revelation that healing power is communicated to a desperate woman through a mere trembling, hesitant, fingertip touch of the fringe on Jesus' robe? We can see that white, frail hand and the teary, hopeful, though frightened eyes focused on the hem of Jesus' clothes. How is it that an ailment of twelve years' duration, the ebbing of her life blood itself, is stanched without Jesus even having knowledge of her presence, much less speaking to her? And how is this healing, which seems to occur almost mechanically, experienced by Jesus as a flow of power from himself to another, alerting him to the fact that, though he did not observe it directly, someone has touched him? Why is physical contact between Jesus and this woman so powerfully life-changing? Again, we can only guess at the answers. But on the basis of what we already know about Jesus, we can make some informed guesses that are more than mere stabs in the dark.

As the one absolutely committed to living in God's world house and drawing others into that household, Jesus is a pregnant source of hope for all who encounter him. Whatever has diminished life for them, made it painful or small, gives way to the vision which Jesus himself embodies. This man, the bleeding woman knows, is different. Whereas doctors have failed to offer her a cure, this compelling figure whose face and voice, whose very movements, promise fresh life and freedom from all manner of disease, is *himself embodied hope!* She touches his clothing, and her faith that things will change for her makes it so. Furthermore, I think that we can speculate that Jesus felt the exchange between them precisely *because she also gave something back to him.* Genuine reciprocity has happened. Does he not say as much when he tells her that it is her faith that has made her well? He has been the grateful *recipient of her trust.* Many, no doubt, had jostled against him in the press of the crowd. But she had touched him with intention and hopeful trust. So doing, she has given to him, as well, a precious gift, even as he returns a priceless gift to her. Something truly human and healing *for them both* has occurred in this exchange. Both have received a pledge of peace thereby. They have been brother and sister in God's world house and opened a window for the rest of us who interlace our stories with theirs.

Rose of Sharon's story is in some ways like the hemorrhaging woman's. Perhaps this woman's flow of blood began with a miscarried pregnancy, or, like Rose of Sharon, perhaps she suffered the still birth of a child. In any case, both women are forlorn creatures, needing healing and restoration amidst crushing loss. Rose gives to another human sufferer out of the searing pain of her own suffering and preserves his life, even as her dead baby's body lies in its new, pitiful grave. Who would have believed that the hemorrhaging woman in Luke 8 had anything to give to Jesus? Out of her overwhelming pain, though, she gives to Jesus—needful of human community as much as she—the incomparable gift of trust, confidence in him and all that he is and his healing power in relation to her. Has anyone ever received a greater gift from another? In fact, is Jesus' gift of physical healing any greater than her gift to him? His joyous response to her acknowledges the value of her gift to his well being; she is not the only one whose welfare has been enhanced. "Daughter, your faith has made you well; go in peace." I wonder why the translators have not placed an exclamation point at the end of Jesus' statement! Surely it is spoken amid wreaths of smiles and dancing eyes looking into other dancing eyes! How could it be otherwise?! Let us not efface the celebrative community these two share at such a sacred moment. God's house resounds with their jubilation!

In extolling Jesus as the great giver of life, we have not always recognized that he was the one truly able to receive from others as well. So doing, we have courted the docetic error and cheated ourselves. Jesus teaches us to receive as well as to give. Here, in this encounter with a suffering woman, Jesus is not afraid to be needy with her. Hierarchy does not call the shots. Secure in himself, his genius, his art, his commitment to God and God's house, Jesus can be fully human, needing others' love and trust even as they need his love and healing. His ministry is not a one-way street. All whom he engages he also needs and receives from as well. Indeed, Jesus' gifts and genius are born and nurtured in community with others just as ours are. That is why he stays behind in the temple in that twelfth year. That is why he announces his mission to the hometown neighbors who have worshiped with him and nurtured him in synagogue all his growing-up years. That is why he calls to himself a company of men and women who walk his journey with him. Now, he needs this hemorrhaging woman's touch and its confirmation of trust and confidence.

How does the story of this woman's gift of trust to Jesus connect to the thesis I am setting forth? Its connection is at the point of community and the nature of incarnational gift-giving as a communal reality. Jesus, like other humans, does not merely give to others, but he, like us all, receives as gift what he needs from others. *Babette's Feast* can again help us to grasp this point. Babette does not merely give her culinary genius to others; she receives from them the acceptance and appreciation of her gift which both validate and expand it. For that reason, her days in Berlevaag now come to fulfillment. For that reason, also, she will not return to Paris where those who received her gift in bygone days are no longer there to respond reciprocally to her genius. *In community* gift is given and received and reciprocity is itself experienced as gift. The woman in Luke 8 has the capacity to trust and to give the gift of trust. That gift also requires self-sacrifice and self-expression. Its self-sacrificial nature inheres in its requirement of risk and vulnerability. Its self-expression occurs in courageous acts like the bleeding woman's assertive, though hesitant, touch of Jesus' robe. Psychologists know the profound nature of trust and its complex and significant origin and mode of nurture *within community*. The Lukan narrative captures this deep truth and transmits it to us.

Like Babette, Jesus has needed those who could receive his great genius, including those who would seek later to kill him. Refusing to separate enemies from friends (again like Babette), Jesus pours himself out for all the community, using his final breath on the cross to plead for their forgiveness.

Let us interlace these stories with that of Jesus' interaction with another woman, the woman at the well near Sychar. As John begins this story, he tells us that Jesus is exhausted and thirsty. A

56

Samaritan woman approaches the well, and Jesus asks her to give him a drink of water. She is surprised for multiple reasons that he makes this request of her. For one thing, Jews do not talk to Samaritans, much less drink from their vessels. Second, even if they did, they still would not talk to a Samaritan woman. Furthermore, he has made a request of her, putting himself in the position of a supplicant, in a sense, her subordinate. And she must be struck by his manner. Again, Jesus displays the self-assurance and gentleness that come only from one who likes and is comfortable with himself. Most surprising of all is the topic of conversation which he chooses. Moving quickly beyond ordinary matters like Jewish-Samaritan social relations, Jesus engages her in a theological discussion. Soundly confusing her with a spirited dialogue about living water, Jesus does not let up. He honors her by talking with her about the nature of worship, assuring her that where one worships, whether on the mountain or in Jerusalem, will finally be revealed as immaterial. In a tacit manner, Jesus is again raising the issue of what it means, in terms of attitude and behavior, to dwell in God's house. Worship which is true and thereby of the Spirit characterizes the praise of the inhabitant of God's house. By including despised Samaritans, Jesus is modeling true worship. By deeming a Samaritan woman a worthy theological disputant, he is modeling true worship. Once more, Jesus is being fully himself, engaging, brilliant, self-confident, expressing his genius without false humility. When the woman mentions the Messiah who, on his coming, will proclaim all things, Jesus unhesitatingly replies: "I am he, the one who is speaking to you." We remember Babette's similarly unhesitating reply to Martine and Philippa: "I am a great artist." There is nothing of braggadocio in the words of either of these artists. They *are* all that they claim.

Because Jesus expresses all that he is, the Samaritan woman is enabled to move toward her own liberation and self-expression. We are not told much more about her, but we feel confident that she will not continue her unhappy pattern of seeking herself in one destructive and disappointing liaison after another. His freedom engenders her freedom. John's deft narrative touch inscribed in the phrase, "then the woman left her water jar . . . ," subtly tells the reader that the overflow of living water from Jesus to this woman has set her on her own rich narrative journey (John 4:28).

Like Jesus, Babette enables the liberation of the unhappy guests at her banquet because her own liberated spirit has conveyed itself through her marvelous cuisine. Freedom truly expressed begets freedom and further true expression. John's biblical story shows it, and so does Dinesen's.

Allow me to illustrate by interlacing a part of my story. For the first three of my seven and one-half years on the Southeastern Baptist Theological Seminary faculty, I seldom ventured a word in faculty meetings. Negotiating introversion has been a life-long task for me. One member of our faculty, however, in the autumn of 1987, during the time of the Fundamentalist takeover at Southeastern, began to stand out as leader, speaker, champion of academic and religious freedom. This person was Richard Hester. Gradually, as Dick grew in confidence in expressing his significant gifts, I found my own voice emerging, my thoughts sharpening, and my reserve crumbling. Dick Hester's freedom helped evoke my own liberation. Several colleagues noticed the change in me. Like Babette's silent guests and Jesus' taciturn well companion, I began to warm to the genius truly expressed in relation to me and those around me. And like those guests and the Samaritan woman, I was changed, too, transformatively, creatively. Christlike in his own powers and their expression, Dick Hester was an embodied agent of graceful transformation. Daring to put himself forward courageously, confidently, sure of his gifts, Dick Hester contagiously helped me and others to set out on a like journey. Many of us left our water jars and went into the city. And others of us frolicked in the snow, falling, regaining our balance, laughing with a glee we had almost forgotten, calling out to our companions, "Bless you! Bless you! Bless you!" The lights in the windows of God's house beckoned us to jubilation.

Jubilation. Let us continue to attend to this theme of jubilation. Jesus the Jubilant is a person we scarcely know, but the fault has been ours, not the evangelists'. John's depiction of Jesus at the marriage at Cana shows us a convivial, celebrative wedding guest, fully entering into the frivolity and enlarging it with his own expansive genius. We need now to interlace the Cana narrative with those we already have. Jesus who sacrifices his gifts for the purpose of expanding and populating God's house is one who celebrates the goodness of life lived in God's house. He feels and expresses jubilation and beckons others to do the same. The story is told in John 2:1–11.

Western Christians have not seen clearly enough jubilation in the personality and behavior of Jesus. We have painted him as victor, judge, lord, king, prophet, priest, and reconciler, but we have seen far too dimly and painted far too hesitantly Jesus the celebrant, the jubilant. Can that be one reason, maybe a major reason, the church is attracting fewer and fewer adherents today? Do people need to celebrate, to be jubilant, perhaps almost as much as they need food, acceptance, and physical health? Have we not left something crucial out of the picture of Jesus which the church gives to the world, at least in large part? Have we reduced the gospel thereby? I am inclined to think so.

Our perspective can be sharpened by interlacing the story of another wedding reception with that of the celebration at Cana. A few years ago, I attended the wedding of Susan, my older daughter Beth's best friend. It was in May at Nag's Head on North Carolina's outer banks, and the wedding reception was held beside the Atlantic at a beautiful but chilly place. Beth and many of the younger adults there had just completed three years of law school and were now pouring on the grueling study needed to prepare themselves for the bar exam in July. This weekend was to be the sole exception to their regimen of study. I knew how demanding the three years of law school had been for them all and how hard they were working to ready themselves for that dreaded bar exam. But as I watched Beth and her friends take to the dance floor, champagne glasses in hand, I witnessed a shining, wonderful transformation. Those tired law graduates danced like gleeful children, cavorting about the floor, laughter ringing over the sounds of the dance band. Their long hours of hard work were for a time put aside and re-creation became a reality. Jubilation over the wedding, yes, but more than that, jubilation for the goodness of life, the fun and joy of life, was what all of us felt, young and old alike.

Is this what the story of the marriage at Cana is about? I think we have sifted too much human celebration out of this story in our efforts to understand and interpret it. In any case, we can see that Jesus entered with abandon the glee and jubilation of the event, filling the wine jars to overflowing with the best of wines.

Though John does not tell us so, I would venture a guess that Jesus danced and cavorted and laughed, wine cup in hand, putting aside for a time the demands of his important ministry and the hard work he would resume on the morrow. And because he entered into the jubilation with gusto, others were caught up in the gaiety, as well.

Where else do the scriptures show us a jubilant Jesus? How about the triumphal entry into Jerusalem at the time of the Passover festival? Why have we so often missed the celebrative Jesus here? Is it because we know what comes next? Perhaps. But let us stay awhile and interlace this story with the others and see if the dancing, celebrating Jesus at Cana cannot be identified here, as well.

> When they were approaching Jerusalem, at Bethphage and Bethany, near the Mount of Olives, he sent two of his disciples and said to them, "Go into the village ahead of you, and immediately as you enter it, you will find tied there a colt that has never been ridden; untie it and bring it. If anyone says to you, 'Why are you doing this?' just say this, 'The Lord needs it and will send it back here immediately.'" They went away and found a colt tied near a door, outside in the street. As they were untying it, some of the bystanders said to them, "What are you doing, untying the colt?" They told them what Jesus had said; and they allowed them to take it. Then they brought the colt to Jesus and threw their cloaks on it; and he sat on it. Many people spread their cloaks on the road, and others spread leafy branches that they had cut in the fields. Then those who went ahead and those who followed were shouting,
>
> > "Hosanna!
> > Blessed is the one who comes in
> > the name of the Lord!
> > Blessed is the coming kingdom
> > of our ancestor David!
> > Hosanna in the highest Heavens!" (Mark 11:1–10)

Surely we are not to imagine that Jesus sat silent and unsmiling as the crowds sang and praised God! Despite what we have often and truly been told about the fickleness of this crowd of celebrants, at this moment their actions are sincere, if ill-informed. With branches and cloaks strewn before him, and men, women, and children shouting their blessings and delight, Jesus must have reciprocated with laughter and joyous waves of his arms to these people honoring him so loudly and vigorously. Again, as at Cana, celebration is the mood, and we need to experience the jubilant side of Jesus as fully as the gospel story presents it to us.

The revelers shout: "Blessed is the coming kingdom of our ancestor David!" Let us digress a bit and interlace a story from the Hebrew scriptures. Although including the story here is somewhat of an intrusion, perhaps, it is relevant, and David's name is central to the goings-on described in Mark's narrative. We are reminded of David's own jubilant dance before the Ark:

> It was told King David, "The Lord has blessed the household of Obed-edom and all that belongs to him, because of the ark of God." So David went and brought up the ark of God from the house of Obed-edom to the city of David with rejoicing; and when those who bore the ark of the Lord had gone six paces, he sacrificed an ox and a fatling. David danced before the Lord with all his might; David was girded with a linen ephod. So David and all the house of Israel brought up the ark of the Lord with shouting, and with the sound of the trumpet.
>
> As the ark of the Lord came into the city of David, Michal daughter of Saul looked out of the window, and saw King David leaping and dancing before the Lord; and she despised him in her heart.
>
> They brought in the ark of the Lord, and set it in its place, inside the tent that David had pitched for it; and David offered burnt offerings and offerings of well-being before the Lord. When David had finished offering the burnt offerings and the offerings of well-being, he blessed the people in the name of the Lord of hosts, and distributed food among all the people, the whole multitude of Israel, both men and women, to each a cake of bread, a portion of meat, and a cake of raisins. Then all the people went back to their homes.
>
> David returned to bless his household. But Michal the daughter of Saul came out to meet David, and said, "How the king of Israel honored himself today, uncovering himself today before the eyes of his servants' maids, as any vulgar fellow might shamelessly uncover himself!" David said to Michal, "It was before the Lord, who chose me in place of your father and all his household, to appoint me as prince over Israel, the people of the Lord, that I have danced before the Lord. I will make myself yet more contemptible than this, and I will be abased in my own

eyes; but by the maids of whom you have spoken, by them I shall be held in honor." And Michal the daughter of Saul had no child to the day of her death. (2 Samuel 6:12–23)

Michal's rancor toward David prevents her from celebrating with the people and her husband and household. No doubt, David's leaping and dancing flipped his linen ephod this way and that, exposing the kingly attributes to one and all. An insecure, childless wife might understandably focus more on that fact than her husband's jubilant exultation, but we feel sorry for her and grieve with her over her failure to leap and dance with him, as well as over her childlessness and the unhappiness of their marriage.

Let us interlace a part of the church's story. Leaping and dancing were aspects of worship at New Light Free Will Baptist Church in Bladenboro, North Carolina, when I was growing up. We lived in Bladenboro until I was seven, and I remember my mother and friends of hers like Miss Delphie Carter whirling around the church floor in jubilation. They called it shouting. Worship at New Light Baptist was anything but somber on those occasions. It was exciting! I recall as a pre-school child sitting under the collection table and watching the grown-ups dance before the Lord. Over the years, I have interpreted their experience in various ways. Now, I am inclined to think they had something we have lost. Yes, they were poor, economically oppressed mill workers, and I can understand that their worship included psychological release from the stark circumstances they faced daily, even as it did for black slaves in their "hush harbors" a century earlier, but that explanation is reductionistic if made to carry the full weight. More was happening at New Light Baptist than catharsis. Joy, thanksgiving, exultation, *jubilation* were happening! Mind and body, spirit and matter, were joined in an ecstatic leap and dance of worship of God who loves and sustains through *all* life's weary journey, God who gives the dawn and twilight, the soft soil and falling rains, the red tomatoes hanging on their pungent, green stalks, and the block of ice wrapped in burlap on the back porch waiting to chill Saturday's and Sunday's iced tea. This was my mother's God, before whom she danced. This was the God who lifted her from her bed of infection after her second baby died and reminded her that, though she could never bear another child, she still had a curly-haired two-year-old waiting for her to get well.

Like David, my mother connected dancing in jubilation before the Lord with making offerings, blessing others, and feeding the hungry. Sunday morning and evening shouting at New Light Baptist was of a piece with Monday and Tuesday morning blessing of the Butler children and handing her mustard biscuits out the back porch screen door to Charlie and Mae Butler's eight hungry offspring. Untying her embroidered, white handkerchief as the collection plate was passed around, my mother dropped quarters and nickels and dimes and an occasional paper bill into the shiny, metal plate. That was her tithe for the money she made as a winder in the cotton mill at the end of our street. Shouting, whirling, dancing, tithing, blessing, feeding, my mother lived a jubilant Christian story.

Again, I wonder if the declining number of people in our churches has anything to do with a decline in jubilation. Might basketball and football games, rock concerts, wedding receptions, and beach parties, be so very attractive because they offer the chance to be jubilant? And why not? But would it not be wonderful to feel the jubilation of dancing and leaping before the Ark with David or whirling and shouting before the Lord with my mother and Delphie Carter?

In whatever form we can get jubilation back into worship, it might serve us and God's world house well for us to do so. The old Brothers and Sisters at Babette's feast leave the party in jubilant spirit, playing in the snow, blessing one another through shrieks of laughter. Might it be that jubilation naturally precedes both blessing others and, as with David and my mother, distributing food to them? David danced and blessed the people and distributed bread, meat, and cakes of raisins to them. My mother shouted and blessed and gave to Eunice, Devola, and their brothers and sisters homemade biscuits spread with French's mustard.

Elisabeth Moltmann-Wendel, in her book *A Land Flowing With Milk and Honey*, quotes Erich Fromm's observation that all mothers generally manage somehow to give their children milk. But only a happy (jubilant) mother is able to give her child honey (Moltmann-Wendel, 1988). Has the church as birthing and nurturing mother preached and taught a gospel with adequate milk but too little honey because we have dissected too much of the leaping and dancing, the jubilation and shouting, from the Jesus Story? Certainly, jubilation is in the pages of the Gospels, at Cana, entering Jerusalem, wherever Jesus talks about joy and abundant life and lives it before and with the people. It behooves us to declaim the exhortatory words of the prophet, the solemn and comforting words of the priest, *and* the celebratory words of the worshiper, remembering and enjoying the richness of the treasure God has entrusted to us. According to the biblical story and other stories, the plot progression might well be from jubilation, to offering, to blessing, to giving and feeding. Perhaps the correction of *many* of our social ills, including hunger and more, awaits our jubilation to start the process.

What can we learn from the baptized community of celebrants at the Lord's Table at New Light Baptist Church? Not necessarily that we should express our joy through shouting, as they did those years ago, but that the gospel *is* jubilant and that true worship will be, at least on important occasions, *celebrative and ecstatic*. We can trustingly risk losing ourselves in it, standing outside ourselves in jubilation. We can also learn to *preach* a jubilant gospel and to value joy and happiness along with sobriety and seriousness. Those values need not be in conflict, as we have too often acted as though they were. Christianity might become more attractive to certain others if the church were not always raining on their parade. This certainly does not argue for mindless hedonism or foolish disregard for integrity in any form. Rather, it acknowledges that jubilation is a valuable part of multiple aspects of life—friendship, parenting, sexual relations, enjoyment of and regard for nature, work and play, justice and peace action, and the Duke Blue Devils winning the NCAA national basketball championship two years in a row! The God who gives to us in Christ abundant joy has made us capable of laughter and exhilaration. These, too, glorify the Creator of all that is.

As we follow the Jesus Story, we could look at many more stories within the larger story, and we shall look at others in parts II and III of this book, but let us move now to the passion story and interlace it with all that we have done. Here the red thread completes its design. From that first visit as a boy to the Jerusalem temple to this last encounter with the high priest, Jesus has followed a consistent journey. From then until now, he has known where he was going: into his Father's house. And he has known why he was going there: to open its doors to the hungry, grieving, rejected, sick, imprisoned, lonely, sinful and repentant, and to those who seek peace and practice just and loving relations, *and* to those who wish to jubilate and celebrate the joy and goodness of life in God's house.

Jesus has known, too, at least for some time, that his journey could, and in all likelihood would, end in his death. His living sacrifice will end in an ultimate sacrifice of life itself. He is ready for that, though he does not seek it nor wish it; the scene in Gethsemane shows that this is so. Yet nothing will deflect him from his course. His commitment and resolve are ultimate, absolute. He will withstand mocking, beating, abuse, and finally crucifixion for the sake of that which is ultimately, infinitely valuable—life here and hereafter in the household of God.

> Now Jesus stood before the governor; and the governor asked him, "Are you the King of the Jews?" Jesus said, "You say so." But when he was accused by the chief priests and elders, he did not answer. Then Pilate said to him, "Do you not hear how many accusations they make against you?" But he gave him no answer, not even to a single charge, so that the governor was greatly amazed.
>
> Then the soldiers of the governor took Jesus into the governor's headquarters, and they gathered the whole cohort around him. They stripped him and put a scarlet robe on him, and after twisting some thorns into a crown, they put it on his head. They put a reed in his right hand and knelt before him and mocked him, saying, "Hail, King of the Jews!" They spat on him, and took the reed and struck him on the head. After mocking him, they stripped him of the robe and put his own clothes on him. Then they led him away to crucify him. (Matthew 27:11–14, 27–31)

Jesus' supreme self-composure and self-definition enrage his tormentors. Attempting to mock him with a scarlet robe and a crown of thorns, they are mocked instead. He will not deny who he is, his genius, his great artistry, his inviolable relationship to God. We hear him again in the Nazareth synagogue: "This day this prophecy has been fulfilled in your hearing." His messianic mission nearly accomplished, he stands now before his interrogators quietly self-assured, a paradigm of self-sacrifice on the highest level. Having repeatedly reiterated in word and deed what he had told his mother in the temple years ago and the hometown folk in Nazareth, Jesus has nothing more to say. He has said in countless ways, "I am a great artist." What else could Babette Hersant say? What more can Jesus say?

Isak Dinesen's story of Babette's feast has been helpful for enabling us to lift out some aspects of the nature of Jesus' self-sacrifice which theologians have often, perhaps most often, obscured. It is at this point, however, that the biblical story stands forth most clearly as the normative, paradigmatic story. Babette's sacrifice is not an ultimate one, neither in terms of where it ends for her personally nor in terms of its effect on Dinesen's readers. Jesus' sacrifice, on the other hand, is a sacrifice unto personal death, and its effect on readers and hearers of the gospel story is unique, the channel of restoration and reconciliation to God and others. It is a source of transformation and new life, new hope, indeed, new habitation in God's own house. Readers and hearers are drawn into the gospel story to become characters in the story itself, living life according to its plot. Dinesen's marvelous story, as good as it is, does not draw its readers inside the text with this power, transforming their very lives and setting them on a new course. It is for this reason that we read Dinesen's story in light of the gospel story, though a genuine reciprocity, an interlacing, occurs which sheds helpful illumination on the biblical story as well. We recognize Babette as a Christ-like figure. We do not interpret Jesus as a Babette-like figure. Nonetheless, because she is like him, and Rose of Sharon is like him, we understand Jesus better as a result. The continuing incarnation in these figures, partial but true, enlarges our perspective and augments our apprehension of the particular incarnation of God in Jesus of Nazareth.

Let us attempt a brief summary of our study up to this point. To do so, we need to return to Dietrich Bonhoeffer's central question and add some questions of our own. Who is Jesus Christ for us today? What Christology shall the church proclaim? What does the Jesus Story tell us? What is true, life-giving, redemptive? To frame our question from James McClendon's perspective, what must the church teach about Christ if it is to be the church? And to frame it as I have in my classes, what shall we teach about Jesus Christ that will enable the church's faithful discipleship? What vision of Christ is true and *thereby* attractive for contemporary people? I have not attempted an exhaustive Christology in these pages, only a narrative Christology which sheds some storied insight for moving toward answering our questions.

Interlacing biblical stories and other stories literary, biographical, autobiographical, and ecclesial, we have discovered some things. Jesus Christ for us today is one whose great art, whose consummate genius, is self-sacrificially expressed through identification with the poor, hungry, oppressed, sick, outcast, and lonely, the peace loving and justice-building ones, the celebrative and life-loving ones. And he is one who teaches, preaches, and heals to that end, drawing all into the household of God. In penultimate and partial ways, Rose of Sharon, Daniel Coulombe, and Babette Hersant teach, heal, forgive, feed, liberate, celebrate, and wage peace. Jesus does so completely and ultimately. The literary characters are faithful though incomplete pictures of Christ. Their Christlike, redemptive words and actions change those around them; speaking and acting, they are proximate, illuminative reflections of Jesus of Nazareth. They give of their best genuinely and sacrificially.

Jesus' ultimate art and gift, however, are more than teaching, healing, forgiving, feeding, peacemaking, celebrating, and liberating; they are himself as God's incarnation of grace and love. He is God's loving grace become enfleshed in humankind within history. Overcoming the divine/human dualism through his own person, Jesus rejects other dualisms of spirit and matter, friend and foe, heaven and earth, joy and pain, death and resurrection. Journeying toward the cross and death at the hands of his executioners, Jesus carries his commitment and self-sacrifice through to ultimate expression, and thereby gives himself to all humanity and all creation for all time. In Jesus, we see that *genuine self-sacrifice is intense and true life even unto death.*

Self-sacrifice is a narrative of vigorous life lived toward but not for death. Orthodox and popular notions of self-sacrifice have focused on the end of that process and not enough on the nature of the journey itself. For that reason, self-sacrifice has been misunderstood in the manner of ascetics of all eras, including the Lutherans in Dinesen's story. Christians have not clearly enough, often enough, seen that the death of self-sacrifice rightly comes after the *life* of self-sacrifice. First life, then death. First, life lived vigorously, richly, committedly, unreservedly, stumbling and rising, in other words, sacrificially. Only so does one travel the road modeled by Jesus the Christ.

Still, it would be misleading to suggest that only extraordinarily gifted ones like Babette, or a Beethoven or Rembrandt, a Shakespeare or Jane Austen, or Jesus himself, can live a life and die a death of true self-sacrifice. There are many genuine forms of self-sacrifice and many genuine sacrifices. We have already seen this in Rose of Sharon. Ill-educated, poor, certainly no artist in any way we commonly define the term, Steinbeck's character nonetheless models life profoundly lived, sacrificially enabling the survival of another suffering human being. There are more commonplace forms of self-sacrifice than the experience of the uncommonly gifted person like Dinesen's Babette. There is the self-sacrifice of senators like Terry Sanford who risk political death to oppose war with its human and ecological destruction. That is a genuine asceticism and a true self-sacrifice. There are working class fathers and African American mothers who work two and three jobs to educate their children. That is self-sacrifice. None of these exemplars are people who live life disengaged from the common, daily struggle. They are all examples of life lived intensely unto but not for death. In partial ways they reflect the reality of Christ.

We need to conclude this section by giving some attention to the destructive consequences of what has too often passed for the christic model of self-sacrifice. Here I speak of that so-called self-denial that never allows the person to be his or her true self. Women have suffered untold loss at the pagan altar of this kind of self-sacrifice. Men and women of dark skin have as well, as have the poor of all colors and both sexes. And *nature has been sacrificed* according to this same model. For the sake of the few, and at the expense of the many, life has been forfeited, poured out in work that supports the powerful and mighty, sacrificed to others' agendas, or in T. S. Eliot's immortal thought, measured out in coffee spoons (Eliot, 1951). One is not to aspire to create and excel for oneself and the joy and jubilation of developing and expressing one's gifts.

What we have just examined denies the validity of this destructive notion of self-sacrifice. Jesus' self-expenditure, and Babette's, show us that the truth lies elsewhere. Focused outward, toward abundant and rich life—just, peaceful, celebrative life—

faithful self-sacrifice recognizes symbiosis and interconnected-ness at the heart of reality. This christic self-sacrifice evokes the richest gifts, richly developed, of all. The poor, people of color, women, and the earth itself are not diminished and consumed for the sake of the wielders of power and their exclusive and oppressive agendas.

Let us turn, now, to a consideration of narrative Christology and the relation of story and doctrinal theology. A more rigorous theological reflection on the church's central doctrinal questions needs our attention at this point.

Narrative Christology:
Doctrinal Theology and Story

Christian theologians and the church itself have understood, interpreted, and articulated variously the central Christological question of faith. Over the Christian centuries, that pivotal question has been phrased as: "What does it mean to say that Jesus of Nazareth is the Christ?" "What does it mean to say that Jesus is both human and divine?" "Who is Jesus Christ for us today?" There are other forms of this question, all sharing a common faith assumption that Jesus of Nazareth is the Christ of God, both human and divine, and that humankind is redeemed through him.

Companion to the central question of Jesus' human-divine identity is that of the Incarnation and its meaning and nature. Christian theology endeavors to examine, grasp, and communicate this mystery of grace in a form relevant to the time, place, and culture of those to whom it is proclaimed. Much light has been shed on this great mystery from biblical narrative and the church's doctrinal tradition. Still more light waits to be shed in this day and in this place in human-ecological history. I propose that interlacing the story/stories of Jesus from the Christian scriptures with *Babette's Feast* tells us more about what it means for Jesus to be both truly human and truly divine and shines new light on the central mystery of Incarnation.

In what follows, I will pick up the question of how interlacing the biblical narratives with *Babette's Feast* and other stories in the context of worship and discipleship speaks new meaning for the

69

church's doctrinal theology, pointing its teaching in fresh avenues of thought and practice.

The Incarnation and Jesus' Humanity and Divinity

The Nazareth inauguration story discloses what the Incarnation entails. The biblical narrative begins a story of struggle which centers around this very issue. This fact of struggle had already been foreshadowed, in part, by the story of the boy in the temple; his staying behind to dialogue with the teachers had occasioned inconvenience for his family and neighbors and some conflict for him and Mary and Joseph. Now, however, the synagogue incident in Nazareth draws the lines clearly. Incarnation, God's entry into human-ecological history in the person of this Jesus, means certain particular and difficult things. A journey is waiting; a road must be traveled; and a plot surprisingly composed of both self-sacrifice and self-expression waits to be enacted. A wilderness must straightway be entered and, after intense struggle, left again, revisited periodically, and left yet again, until the final wilderness scene in Gethsemane and Jesus' last internal struggle to resist the temptation to exit the God-story. Incarnation classically understood and understood newly today has to do with high drama, life-and-death action, resolute commitment, and all that goes with it. Traditional theological conundrums regarding substance and essence, "stuff", evoke little interest and command little authority today. For today's faithful, the mystery of the Incarnation is graspable at the intersection of Bible, worship, discipleship, and human-ecological story(ies). The Nazareth inauguration story is the contemporary starting point, not the Lukan birth narrative. The inauguration narrative clarifies in precise terms what Incarnation looks like, played out through the elements of plot, character, and setting. Jesus willingly becomes the premier participant in a divine-human narrative, living at one and the same time, truly, concurrently, inseparably, and fully the story of God and the story of humankind. Jesus, as the incarnation of God, is the one who fulfills the Isaiahan prophecy: "today this prophecy is fulfilled." In the Nazareth synagogue Jesus' character is explicitly identified. The *dramatis personae* of God's redemption drama has its protagonist; other characters will soon be added. This dramatic story has a specific, content-filled plot to develop and enact. That, too, is clearly spelled out by the Nazarene protagonist himself: the plot will develop by feeding the hungry, visiting the sick, welcoming the stranger, forgiving the neighbor's debt, restoring his inheritance to him, and valuing truly and rightly all God's creation. As God in human flesh, Jesus the Nazarene proclaims before his family and neighbors gathered for worship in the synagogue this synopsis of the God-human story now unfolding. Immediately and violently rejected for his arrogant claims, Jesus enters the wilderness struggle, equipped by the Spirit of God first to struggle and then to prevail. He emerges blessed, though like Jacob his Hebrew predecessor, wounded and bearing the marks of his battle with the dark angel, the temptation not to follow the narrative journey before him. Thus we see that incarnation, enfleshment, has to do with narrative journeying, not with DNA and other biological data and issues. Jesus' incarnational journey is to the household of God and God's table of hospitality for those named in the synagogue reading from Isaiah: the sick, hungry, rejected, poor, outcast, and all who seek to heal their hurt.

Christian theology has classically preferred the monarchical images in scripture; thus, the destination of the Christian journey has most often been imaged metaphorically as the kingdom of God. While that image is certainly strong in the sacred writings, it is not the monolithic master image the church has traditionally interpreted it to be. Strongly present, as well, is the image of God's house, as this book has already displayed. Now, we see more clearly that God's creation-redemption-consummation plot is a liberating, justice-making, narrative plot unfolding the story of God's grace in the household of God. Jesus lives the plot to its self-sacrificial conclusion, the conclusion of death on a cross. As I have shown by interlacing the Jesus story with *Babette's Feast*, Jesus sacrifices himself in the paradoxical act of owning who he is, in his giftedness, most fully. His rich genius is both expressed and offered extravagantly, truly and fully, for the purpose of opening the doors of God's house to all those whose hearts and spirits yearn to enter. Incarnation is story-living. It is God's story-living and humanity's story-living. Jesus is the incarnation of God because he lives God's story and humanity's story truthfully, concurrently, inseparably, christically, and fully, and thereby peoples the house of God and extends its hospitality to the repentant

71

sinful, the downtrodden and desperate, to each and all alike. Because Jesus of Nazareth is the enfleshment of God on the stage of human-ecological history, grace abounds: lives are restored; the future is opened to God's creative, loving purposes; and hope endures and sustains the hopeless and ravaged, including a ravaged creation.

I have discussed the narrative elements of character and plot in relation to the Christian doctrines of Incarnation and the humanity and divinity of Jesus. Something remains to be said about the narrative element of setting. Theological reflection today is uniquely constrained to engage the topic of narrative *setting* because of several factors, the most obvious and pressing one being that of ecology and planetary ruin. Narrative theological reflection recognizes that characters interact in plots unfolding in concrete historical settings, not in timeless, unlocatable, theoretical "places." The divine-human story unfolds in particular settings, in specific places. What precedes has already suggested where God's story most truly happens. The gospels disclose where this is: in the specific places where the common people throng, hoping to hear a word of hope, a word of forgiveness, a promise of peace—on the treacherous road to Jericho, by a well in hated Samaria, in the house of Simon, inauspicious though that place be, on the side of the road the lepers walk on, in the rooms stinking with the smell of death, and, finally, on the dung heap outside Jerusalem's wall at Calvary. But the Bible also discloses other specific settings we have noted less often: the lonely spot where the sparrow falls, the garden where the lily blooms in radiance and fades, the sea where Leviathan plays, the green pastures where sheep at risk graze protected, the fields of grasses with their cattle, the natural homes of living things and all parts of those sustaining habitats. These are also the places, the settings, where Jesus lives out the divine-human story. The settings themselves are significant, participating symbiotically in the unfolding of the sacred narrative. They sustain with food, air, water, beauty, comfort, with the necessities of life itself. Classical theology and Christology have not adequately expressed the reality that God has, in Jesus, entered the human-*ecological* story. I would propose that Christian theology can no longer responsibly interpret the Bible and the Christian faith without including ecology within Christology. *Where* God's Incarnation story unfolds is important, contributing one of the three vital components of plot, character, and setting. The planet itself and the planetary ecosystem defining Earth are indispensable as the setting of God's Incarnation story of creation, redemption, and promise. Nor does Earth as setting merely function as inert backdrop for the divine-human drama. This implied assumption has been one of Christianity's gravest errors, and one for which the church must admit to its share of liability in the ecological peril the planet faces globally. Setting *participates* in story and has meaning of its own. Most accurately, there is only one meaning for humanity and the rest of nature, a shared meaning of symbiotic interconnection (McClendon, 1994; ch. 4). Present and future theologies cannot omit this truth. God's Incarnation in Jesus the Nazarene, and Jesus' divinity and humanity have to do with God's entry into, not just *human* history, but symbiotic human-ecological setting and story. Interlacing the biblical stories and *Babette's Feast* helps to lift up and focus this truth. Reconciliation and transformation at Babette's hospitality table come through the media of setting and specific, elemental components found and experienced in that specific setting of table fellowship and feasting. Natural elements of food and drink mediate God's grace to dispirited and hostile table companions, transforming them into companions truly. Even Babette's powerful enemy is ministered to and embraced within that grace-mediating setting; thereby the General is also transformed and freed. The interlaced biblical and literary stories show us that symbiotic interconnection is connection with the feared enemy as well. God's Incarnation in Jesus has meaning for overcoming hostility toward nature and human enemies both. This observation points us to our next topic: *atonement*.

Atonement

Much of the task of doctrinal theology, most rightly, concerns itself with analyzing, attempting to understand, and then to express, the nature of God's atoning work in Jesus Christ. Over the Christian centuries, faithful believers who have themselves experienced the transforming grace of atonement have conceptualized this divine work variously as ransom, cosmic victory over Satan, substitutionary death, penal sacrifice, and salvific moral influence. All these conceptions hold some truth, but none is adequate to the task of articulating the central act of God's loving restoration of humankind and creation in oneness. The nature of God's work of "at-one-ment" needs now to be stated with faithfulness for this day and the promise and peril it holds.

A particular biblical passage needs attention for our purposes here. While Scripture holds many expressions of God's atoning activity, the reality of atonement in Jesus Christ is nowhere more clearly expressed than in Ephesians 2:13–22.

> But now in Christ Jesus you who once were far off have been brought near by the blood of Christ. For he is our peace; in his flesh he has made both groups into one and has broken down the dividing wall, that is, the hostility between us. He has abolished the law with its commandments and ordinances, that he might create in himself one new humanity in place of the two, thus making peace, and might reconcile both groups to God in one body through the cross, thus putting to death that hostility through it. So he came and proclaimed peace to you who were far off and peace to those who were near; for through him both of us have access in one Spirit to the Father. So then you are no longer strangers and aliens, but you are citizens with the saints and also members of the household of God, built upon the foundation of the apostles and prophets, with Christ Jesus himself as the cornerstone. In him the whole structure is joined together and grows into a holy temple in the Lord; in whom you also are built together spiritually into a dwelling place for God. (Ephesians 2:13–22)

What atonement is and what it means we can faithfully discern in this profound theological essay from the witness of the early church. Atonement, "at-one-ment", has to do with divine peacemaking, with barrier-breaking and bringing together those who were formerly estranged and hostile. It has to do with making of those separated ones, *one*. Jesus is explicitly called "*our peace*." He is the one who heals our divisions and hatreds, our godless work of stranger-making, and fashions of us all, one new humanity through his ultimate sacrifice on the cross. *Atonement means peace*. Atonement means unity and interconnection. The scandal of Christianity is that atonement means oneness through the body of Jesus hanging on a cross. The consequence of this miracle of peace-and-oneness-making is the *creation of a new household*. As Ephesians clearly states, this is the household of God where there are no strangers and foreigners, only sisters and brothers connected indivisibly by the atoning miracle of God in

74

Christ. What Jesus spent all his working, ministering weeks and months doing, namely, opening the door to God's house and inviting those without to come in, he now does with finality and for all time. His resolution and commitment are forever sealed in a consummate act of *peacemaking* that does not stop short of his own ultimate self-sacrifice. On the cross and through the very flesh of his body itself, Jesus completes his remarkable journey to God's house. The plot has been played out; the narrative has reached its denouement.

While the Ephesians text explicates clearly the atoning work of Christ for a warring humanity, we need to join it with a text from Romans for clarity in seeing the fullness of atonement for all creation. Romans 8 discloses what Christian doctrinal theology has typically tended to overlook: atonement has to do with *all* creation and not the human species alone. Implications for ecological faithfulness and responsibility are striking.

> I consider that the sufferings of this present time are not worth comparing with the glory about to be revealed to us. For the creation waits with eager longing for the revealing of the children of God; for the creation was subjected to futility, not of its own will but by the will of the one who subjected it, in hope that the creation itself will be set free from its bondage to decay and will obtain the freedom of the glory of the children of God. We know that the whole creation has been groaning in labor pains until now; and not only the creation, but we ourselves, who have the first fruits of the Spirit, groan inwardly while we wait for adoption, the redemption of our bodies. For in hope we were saved. Now hope that is seen is not hope. For who hopes for what is seen? But if we hope for what we do not see, we wait for it with patience. (Romans 8:18–25)

Babette's Feast enables us to achieve some degree of clarity also at this point. The Ephesians and Romans texts are illumined when we interlace with them this story. Estranged old women and men are brought near and made one in Dinesen's narrative. Religious allusion indicates the divine source of her characters' remarkable transformation. More subtly stated but there nonetheless is the oneness-making of humankind with the plant and animal creation in communion together at Babette's feast table. Symbiosis and the mutuality of the ecosystem of which all are part play their roles in this subtle and magnificent drama. As in the upper room in Jerusalem, bread and wine, food and drink, become vital,

75

interactive elements in a divine-human-creation drama embracing all, human and not human, as community is healed and reestablished in the mystery of atonement. A more profound oneness than we have dared to believe is mimed for us, both in the biblical narratives and in Dinesen's. It can hardly be coincidental or superfluous that the holy meal of Christianity is exactly that, a meal-taking, a partaking of bread and wine, non-sensate elements of creation symbiotically connected to the women and men who receive them into their bodies as the very flesh and blood of Jesus. Paul declaims the straining and laboring of creation in the divine-human-creation story of world healing and atonement. This is a fact that must claim the church's attention at last. Christian doctrinal theology has much work to do in drawing out the fullness of this amazing and true salvation narrative. In an ecological age, old but new insights cry out for fuller explication that the church might live its life of atonement and faith proclamation more truly and faithfully. At-one-ment, atonement, of humankind *and* the creation may be the church's most sublime proclamation. To be sure, a naturalism pantheistically erasing all lines of distinction need not and cannot be the result. But a true atonement narrative embracing all the creation God originates, shapes, values, and redeems waits to be told theologically. These sentences are a beginning effort at such a telling.

Christological Grace

Dinesen makes the point that grace transforms the wizened, separated members of the little Lutheran fellowship in Berlevaag. In the words of the General that grace is eloquently voiced. But, consistent with Dinesen's style, the Christological nature of that transforming grace is only alluded to; however, it is so amply alluded to that Dinesen's meaning, I propose, is clear. Numerous and striking Christological allusions attest that Dinesen's picture of grace is specifically grace mediated by Christ. Since I have at other places pointed out those several religious allusions and commented briefly on their significance, I will not here repeat them. However, more requires to be said about Christological grace and how the interlacing of *Babette's Feast* and the biblical narratives we have looked at display the nature of that amazing grace. First of all, Isak Dinesen's literary narrative is situated, oriented, in the Christian narrative, shaped in its specific way by the story of God's merciful, loving dealings with Israel, Jesus, and the church. Hers is the story of a Christian fellowship, a small Lutheran body of believers, who have lost the joy of their salvation. In their limited but genuine efforts to live as characters in the story of faith, these elderly saints have tried to follow Christ's way. They have been regular in worship and faithful in witness, and to the extent their waning energies allow, they have persevered diligently in the work of the Lord as they understand it. Their life stories have been shaped by the Story of Jesus, and though they have each missed their lines and forgotten their stage directions, they still attempt to play their roles in that salvation drama. What needs clearer identification is the grace through unstinting self-giving which Babette, like Jesus, embodies on this festive evening.

Perhaps here, more than anywhere else, the power of interlacing is both displayed and needed. Apart from interlacing with the biblical narratives of Jesus, Babette's self-giving endures as a remarkable story of human generosity and courage, but hardly more than that. Dinesen herself, through allusion, interlaces the biblical narratives in the telling of this one, but her understated style is so subtle as to be lost if one does not look closely and also undertake the theological work of interlacing along with the author. If it is that elusive, one might ask, why bother? Is there not enough which is clear and explicit about Christological grace in the scriptural texts alone without bothering with *Babette's Feast* and its obscurity? Yes—and no. The demanding work of listening keenly enough and looking closely enough is rewarded if we are willing to undertake it and persevere. New insights about the enemy as gift emerge from such a labor. And new awareness about grace in and through creation, mediated not naturalistically but Christologically, emerge from the work of interlacing. Possibilities for true and faithful church teaching and doctrine follow in their wake. Therein lies the rationale for undertaking a theological work of this nature. Further possibilities for faithful discipleship also follow and expand the reasons for employing such a methodology. *Babette's Feast* is centrally about atoning grace, and that grace is Christological.

Recoverable Biblical Images
for a Contemporary Christology

The theological-literary method which I designate as interlacing and which I am employing and recommending here holds promise for the recovery of pregnant biblical images for a contemporary Christology. I offer this proposal and intend to develop it by juxtaposing what follows with John Calvin's influential prophet, priest, and king imagery so instrumental in shaping post-Reformation Protestant conceptions. Calvin's triad of images for Christ, re-presenting the structured life of Israel in the life of Jesus, requires some attention to those metaphors here. Calvin's notion is that, in Jesus, the three central elements of the life and history of Israel are joined, redeemed, and fulfilled. In Israel's life, both the metaphors and the concrete work of prophets, priests, and kings had functioned sequentially and, in varying degrees at different times in Israel's history, together. These had operated sometimes in uneasy cooperation and at other times in conflict. In Jesus, Calvin suggests, these three, prophet, priest, and king, are united in harmonious confluence, fulfilling Israel's promise and God's intention.

Since the Reformation, Protestant Christianity has resonated with this imagery and happily adopted it theologically with the result that much modern Christology has advanced the Calvinistic imagery as central to the Christian vision. However, while the images of prophet, priest, and king have functioned with seeming faithfulness for the church in its teaching and discipleship in the past and still do to some extent, they no longer function as convincingly or as faithfully as then. Other images press to replace them, or at least to stand in full authority alongside them. For many in the church today, the metaphors of prophet, priest, and king image a hierarchical progression from the former to the latter, reflecting Israel's own movement in that hierarchical direction, and foster a similar developmental progression (or regression) in the church's life, resulting in a Constantinian understanding and shaping of church. In fact, this movement appears to be exactly what did happen across the Christian centuries. Therefore, to Christians sensitive to this dilemma and concerned about it, other images function more genuinely in enabling the worship, work, and witness of the church in the present day.

The New Testament abounds with Christological images other than Calvin's triad. Prominent among those splendid and evocative images are Jesus the Bread of Life, the Light of the World, the Vine, the Shepherd, the Water of Life, the Door, the Cornerstone, the Body, the Blood, the Lamb of God, our Peace. Scripture images Jesus the Christ through basic elements of the ecosystem—-water, bread, light, stone, vine—-images non-hier-archical and non-elitist, expressing the life of the common folk and their activities of farming, animal husbandry, and house-keeping. Lamentably, these images have tended to languish in the lines of the biblical text with little vitality for engaging the imagi-nation of the church. Why is that so? Many factors account for this state of affairs, no doubt, but one important one, I propose, involves interlacing. Such images capture the imagination of the church *when* we interlace them with biographical stories such as the life of Martin Luther King or Clarence Jordan, or with literary stories such as *Babette's Feast* (McClendon, 1974/1990). Interlacing biblical image with literary image compounds, evidently, the imagistic power resident in the biblical metaphor and impresses it on the reader's psyche. Or, perhaps, it does something like what John Dominic Crossan and Sallie McFague have each described in their studies of biblical parable and metaphor: it shocks the reader into a new awareness, breaking open her "structures of expectation," reorienting her perspective, and opening room for God's Spirit to enter.(Crossan, 1975; McFague, 1975). In interlac-ing, a fresh blowing and breathing of the Spirit happens.

Dinesen's employment of religious allusion, by applying to her protagonist Babette the same images scripture ascribes to Jesus, evokes new awareness otherwise unapprehended by her readers. Her use of biblical, Christological images of the corner-stone, the feast-giver, the filler of wine jars, and the sacrificial servant, and her employment of food and wine as media of transforming grace, suggesting the Last Supper and all Christian sacramental meals thereafter, link compellingly to biblical narra-tives and images familiar to the Christian reader, drawing that one into the space described by Crossan and McFague, a place where something iconoclastic, new, and sacred happens. Thereby the Christian life and the life of the gathered community of the faithful acquire new, or renewed, and fresh definition, conforming to biblical images of servanthood, particularized as feast-giving, hospitality-shaping and peace-making membership in the household of God. Living the Christian story truly—meaning *truthfully*, in the mode Stanley Hauerwas has described so helpfully in his work—requires just such imaginative and imagistic renewal (Hauerwas, 1977; 1981). The theological work of interlacing can revitalize the church's faithfulness so understood. It can also renew and revitalize the church's doctrinal theology.

Let us continue our study by proceeding to part II and stories of the human heart in conflict with itself. Humanity in narrative will be our focus.

Stories of "Problems of the Human Heart in Conflict with Itself"

In William Faulkner's 1950 acceptance speech delivered on the occasion of his acceptance of the Nobel Prize for Literature, Faulkner chose to address his brief remarks to aspiring young writers. In essence, he told them not to write about this or that or the other good (or not so good) thing, but about the one thing finally *worth* writing about—the "problems of the human heart in conflict with itself." In writing about that ubiquitous human struggle the author would, Faulkner believed, attend to "the old verities and truths of the heart, the old universal truths lacking which any story is ephemeral and doomed—love and honor and pity and pride and compassion and sacrifice. Until he does so, he labors under a curse. He writes not of love but of lust, of defeats in which nobody loses anything of value, of victories without hope, and, worst of all, without pity or compassion" (Faulkner, in Cowley, ed., 1946/1987:724).

Faulkner's subject, of course, was the story of humankind itself, the age-old story of creation, fall, and redemption, or, said differently, the universal story of birth, death, and resurrection. This comprehensive narrative will be our focus in this second part of our study. Prior to returning to the biblical narratives for close examination, let us look again at *Babette's Feast* and briefly at other stories within the context of Faulkner's notions. Then, we shall turn to the biblical stories again, allowing an interplay, an interlacing of biblical stories and contemporary stories, a dance of images, insights, awakenings, and tremblings of the heart.

Dinesen's characters—the elderly Brothers and Sisters of the Lutheran sect, Martine and Philippa, Achille Papin, Lorens Loewenhielm, and Babette—all have their particular struggles of the heart. Dinesen guides us through their travail and reveals their defeats and victories, showing us aspects of ourselves and casting illumination on the biblical stories to which we shall turn shortly. At the same time, because we are shaped by the stories of Jacob and David, Esther and Jesus, Dinesen's characters and their strivings are understood in the context of those sacred narratives and particularly, as we have already seen in Part I, in the context of the Jesus Story which for Christians is the story by which we interpret our lives and all of reality.

Before looking specifically at *Babette's Feast* again, we might be enlightened by attending to certain of Dinesen's briefer narratives, contained within her autobiographical work *Out of Africa*, thereby getting some further information about her perspective and life. William Luce's play about Dinesen, *Lucifer's Child*, based on Dinesen's writings, will be helpful as well. In the pages of *Out of Africa*, Dinesen tells a story which she entitles "The Roads of Life." It is reproduced below:

> When I was a child I was shown a picture,—a kind of moving picture inasmuch as it was created before your eyes and while the artist was telling the story of it. This story was told, every time, in the same words.
>
> In a little round house with a round window and a little triangular garden in front there lived a man.
>
> Not far from the house there was a pond with a lot of fish in it.
>
> One night the man was woken up by a terrible noise, and set out in the dark to find the cause of it. He took the road to the pond.
>
> Here the story-teller began to draw, as upon a map of the movements of an army, a plan of the roads taken by the man.
>
> He first ran to the South. Here he stumbled over a big stone in the middle of the road, and a little farther he fell into a ditch, got up, fell into a ditch, got up, fell into a third ditch, and got out of that.
>
> Then he saw that he had been mistaken, and ran back to the North. But here again the noise seemed to him to come from the South, and he again ran back there. He first stumbled over a big stone in the middle of the road, then a little later he fell into a ditch, got up, fell into another ditch, got up, fell into a third ditch, and got out of that.
>
> He now distinctly heard that the noise came from the end of the pond. He rushed to the place, and saw that a big leakage had

been made in the dam, and the water was running out with all the fishes in it. He set to work and stopped the hole and only when this had been done did he go back to bed.

When now the next morning the man looked out of his little round window,—thus the tale was finished as dramatically as possible,—what did he see?—A Stork!

Dinesen comments on the story:

> I am glad that I have been told this story and I will remember it in the hour of need. The man in the story was cruelly deceived, and had obstacles put in his way. He must have thought: "What ups and downs! What a run of bad luck!" He must have wondered what was the idea of all his trials, he could not know that it was a stork. But through them all he kept his purpose in view, nothing made him turn round and go home, he finished his course, he kept his faith. That man had his reward. In the morning he saw the stork. He must have laughed out loud then.
>
> *The tight place, the dark pit in which I am now lying, of what bird is it the talon? When the design of my life is completed, shall I, shall other people see a stork?*
>
> . . . .
>
> You are bewildered when you read the second article of faith of the Christian Church: That He was crucified, dead and buried, that He went down into Hell, and also did rise again the third day, that He ascended into Heaven, and from thence shall come again.
>
> What ups and downs, as terrible as those of the man in the story. What is to come out of all this?—The second article of the Creed of half the world. (Dinesen, 1937/1985:261–63)

This story is important for an understanding of Dinesen herself and an understanding of the meaning of her literary contribution. It reveals that Dinesen strove to understand her personal struggles and those of her characters in the stories she wrote *within the interpretive context of the Jesus Story*, within the interpretive frame of the "second article of the Creed of half the world." Jesus' fallings and risings, the crucifixion and resurrection, Dinesen believed, held the key for humanity's fallings and risings and the possibility of "seeing the stork."

William Luce's play, *Lucifer's Child*, portrays Dinesen's arduous strivings with the trials, the ups and downs, of her own life. There were many. Her adored father killed himself when she was ten. In the first year of her marriage to her cousin, Baron Bror Blixen, she contracted syphilis from him, a ravaging disease from which she suffered horribly for the rest of her life. Her capacity to bear children was destroyed. Her marriage ended in divorce, and the love of her life, Denys Finch-Hatton, never married her. Finch-Hatton was finally killed in a plane crash, and, at last, Dinesen lost her beloved coffee farm in the Ngong Hills of Kenya. Loss and death characterized the narrative of her life. Forced to return to Denmark in 1931, she enlisted the financial support of her brother for two years while she taught herself to write. A storyteller all her life, until that time Karen Dinesen Blixen had not written her stories.

Always impatient with those forces that shrink life, Dinesen was enthralled by the Jacob story. Jacob's refusal to let the angel go unless he blessed him became a formative image, a paradigm, for her own struggles with life. Loss, disease, pain, and death were the stork's talons, dark pits from which she ascended by refusing to release the angel until he had blessed her. Dinesen interlaced the roads of life story with the Jacob story and both of those with her own story to make sense of it all. The blessing came in her own growth in pity, compassion, love, endurance, courage, and sacrifice. And the blessing came through her stories written and lived. This refusal to turn loose of her own experiences of loss and death (and celebration) until she had exacted blessings from them, and then her marvelous freedom to let go truly, is Dinesen's autobiographical source of Babette's wisdom in her short story masterpiece.

In Luce's introduction to *Lucifer's Child*, he quotes his subject: "'The divine art is the story. In the beginning was the story'" (Luce, 1989/1992:vii). As Luce relates, having adopted Isak Dinesen as her literary name, Karen Christentze Dinesen Blixen, upon her return to Denmark "lived out her [remaining] years at Rungstedlung, as ill health gradually took its toll—." Luce continues:

> She described herself as being caught 'in a pit, in a dark place.' She wanted out of the dark place all of her life. Her favorite Bible passage was 'I will not let thee go, except thou bless me'—Jacob's passionate bargain as he struggled with the angel at Peniel. The angel's blessing for Jacob was redemption and the new name, Israel. In her own Peniel experience, Baroness Karen Blixen

wrestled with her dark angel and exacted a similar redemption. She became Isak [Isaac, God has brought laughter] Dinesen, the light-bearing storyteller of the century. (Luce, 1989/1992:viii)

Dinesen's interlacing of the Jacob story with her own life story and that interlacing's function as source for her writing need close examination. In a brief narrative in *Out of Africa*, which Dinesen names with the biblical words themselves, "I Will Not Let Thee Go Except Thou Bless Me," she writes about what she has suffered and endured and from which she has emerged halt but blessed, empowered to live as Isak, one who laughs.

When in Africa in March the long rains begin after four long months of hot, dry weather, the richness of growth and the freshness and fragrance everywhere are overwhelming.

But the farmer holds back his heart and dares not trust to the generosity of nature, he listens, dreading to hear a decrease in the roar of the falling rain. The water that the earth is now drinking in must bring the farm, with all the vegetable, animal and human life on it, through four rainless months to come.

It is a lovely sight when the roads of the farm have all been turned into streams of running water, and the farmer wades through the mud with a singing heart, out to the flowering and dripping coffee-fields. But it happens in the middle of the rainy season that in the evening the stars show themselves through the thinning clouds; then he stands outside his house and stares up, as if hanging himself on to the sky to milk down more rain. He cries to the sky: "Give me enough and more than enough. My heart is bared to thee now, and I will not let thee go except thou bless me. Drown me if you like, but kill me not with caprices. No *coitus interruptus*, heaven, heaven!"

Sometimes a cool, colourless day in the months after the rainy season calls back the time of the *marka mbaya*, the bad year, the time of the drought. In those days the Kikuyu used to graze their cows round my house, and a boy amongst them who had a flute, from time to time played a short tune on it. When I have heard this tune again, it has recalled in one single moment all our anguish and despair of the past. It has got the salt taste of tears in it. *But at the same time I found in the tune, unexpectedly surprisingly, a vigour, a curious sweetness, a song. Had those hard times really had all these in them*? There was youth in us then, a wild hope. *It was during those long days that we were all of us merged into a unity*, so that on another planet we shall recognize one another, and the things cry to each other, the cuckoo clock and

85

my books to the lean-fleshed cows on the lawn and the sorrowful old Kikuyus: "You also were there. You also were part of the Ngong farm." *That bad time blessed us and went away.*

The friends of the farm came to the house, and went away again. They were not the kind of people who stay for a long time in the same place. They were not the kind of people either who grow old, they died and never came back. But they had sat contented by the fire, and when the house, closing round them, said: "I will not let you go except you bless me," they laughed and blessed it, and it let them go.

An old lady sat in a party and talked of her life. She declared that she would like to live it all over again, and held this fact to prove that she had lived wisely. I thought: Yes, her life has been the sort of life that should really be taken twice before you can say that you have had it. An arietta you can take *da capo*, but not a whole piece of music,—not a symphony and not a five-act tragedy either. If it is taken over again it is because it has not gone as it ought to have gone.

My life, I will not let you go except you bless me, but then I will let you go. (Dinesen, 1937/1985:285–87, emphasis added)

This final sentence spoken to her life itself is Isak Dinesen's signature statement. It appears literarily in *Babette's Feast*, through the story Dinesen tells. It is connected to and interlaced with the Jacob story, the Apostles Creed, and the Christian story itself. It affirms that the hard times do, indeed, have curiously within them both anguish and despair *and* a surprising vigor and sweetness, even a song.

Dinesen concludes the roads of life story with an introspective reflection on the Apostles Creed and its reference to Jesus' sufferings and their meaning for the grand drama of human history. *Babette's Feast* can only be understood within this rich, religious context and Dinesen's life-long reflection on it.

Babette herself is Dinesen's alter ego, her literary representation, I believe (Luce has Dinesen say in *Lucifer's Child* that she had an unrealized dream of becoming a great chef in Paris). Babette struggles with the dark angel and prevails. Dinesen does the same. In their own ways, Dinesen's other characters do likewise. One might say that Dinesen knew what Faulkner knew; only the struggles of the human heart in conflict with itself are worth writing about.

The conflicts within the hearts of Dinesen's characters take various forms. Injuries against the neighbor, infidelities in relationships, ungrasped opportunities and forfeited chances, talents not developed, trespasses unforgiven, fears unfaced, lapses of courage and hope, beauty uncelebrated and joy spurned, loss of youth and the body's strength, disease and approaching death—these and other manifestations of the dark angel's presence define the conflict for the men and women in Dinesen's narratives.

Let us recall briefly some of the specific "problems of the human heart in conflict with itself" torturing the figures in *Babette's Feast*. Two of the old women had sinned by slandering each other, thereby injuring a girlhood friend, and had consequently ruined both their chances for marriage, family, and property. For forty years, their conflicted hearts had nursed resentment and guilt, and neither compassion nor forgiveness had emerged from the struggle blessing them and enabling them to release their dark angel. An old Brother had swindled another Brother in a business deal, and the forty-five-year-old injury had stuck in the injured brother's mind "like a deep-seated, festering splinter." A Brother and Sister had years ago been involved in an adulterous liaison and had alternately blamed each other and themselves, becoming yearly more guiltily distant and fearful, worrying, "about the possible terrible consequences, through all eternity, to himself, brought upon him by one who had pretended to hold him dear." Martine had missed her chance for love with the young Lieutenant Loewenhielm, believing that her Christian and daughterly duty was to reside throughout her life in her father's household, assisting him in his pastoral work. As for the Lieutenant himself, a failure of courage and nerve had caused him to lose his own chance for happiness with the woman he longed so to court. Philippa who, like her sister, could not separate her life from her father's, lost both the love of her life, Achille Papin, and her own great talent, a magnificent soprano voice which could have been given to all the world. In each of these instances, inner conflict had failed to yield blessing.

Babette herself had wrestled with her own dark angel through long and desperate nights before her entry into the Dean's household and later as a cook there, displaced from her country and those whom she had loved. For her, however, the striving had yielded a blessing. The dark pit, the tight places of the stork's talons, had swallowed her up, but there she had wrestled with

87

the angel and prevailed. Her life had blessed her, and she could turn loose of it. Let us retrace the track of her journey to get a clearer focus on Babette's triumph. Out of the Paris Commune

> on a rainy June night of 1871, the bell-rope of the yellow house was pulled violently three times. The mistresses of the house opened the door to a massive, dark, deadly pale woman with a bundle on her arm, who stared at them, took a step forward and fell down on the doorstep in a dead swoon. When the frightened ladies had restored her to life she sat up, gave them one more glance from her sunken eyes and, all the time without a word, fumbled in her wet clothes and brought out a letter which she handed to them. (Dinesen, 1953/1988:12)

The letter was Achille Papin's recommendation of Babette Hersant for the sisters' employ. With marvelously ironic understatement, as we have seen, Monsieur Papin had written, "Babette can cook."

Though Dinesen tells us little directly of Babette's struggles of the heart, she gives us revelatory glimpses into this refugee's quiet striving:

> And it happened when Martine or Philippa spoke to Babette that they would get no answer, and would wonder if she had even heard what they said. They would find her in the kitchen, her elbows on the table and her temples on her hands, lost in the study of a heavy black book which they secretly suspected to be a popish prayer-book. Or she would sit immovable on the three-legged kitchen chair, her strong hands in her lap and her dark eyes wide open, as enigmatical and as fatal as a Pythia upon her tripod. At such moments they realized that Babette was deep, and that in the soundings of her being there were passions, there were memories and longings of which they knew nothing at all. (Dinesen, 1953/1988:18)

As we already know, Babette and her husband and son had been members of the Communards, resistance fighters in the Paris Commune. Her husband and son had been killed, and she herself had been forced to flee her beloved Paris and relinquish her life as a renowned and celebrated chef, "the greatest culinary genius of the age." Those quiet, motionless times in the kitchen were, we can surmise, times of striving with the dark angel. Out of that strife, Babette extracted a blessing. Enemies and friends became, in a profound sense, the same; the people who starved the poor and killed her husband and son were also the people who had appreciated and celebrated her genius. Out of the conflict of her heart, Babette wrested forgiveness, courage, endurance, sacrifice, hope, and gratitude for the rich ambiguity of existence. The scene in which Babette expresses her startling, redemptive vision is one of the most powerful in all literary art and bears looking at again and again:

> "But all those people whom you have mentioned," she [Philippa] said, "those princes and great people of Paris whom you named, Babette? You yourself fought against them. You were a Communard! The General you named had your husband and son shot! How can you grieve over them?"
> Babette's dark eyes met Philippa's.
> "Yes," she said, "I was a Communard. Thanks be to God, I was a Communard! And those people whom I named, Mesdames, were evil and cruel. They let the people of Paris starve; they oppressed and wronged the poor. Thanks be to God. I stood upon a barricade; I loaded the gun for my menfolk! But all the same, Mesdames, I shall not go back to Paris, now that those people of whom I have spoken are no longer there." She stood immovable, lost in thought. "You see, Mesdames," she said, at last, "those people belonged to me, they were mine. They had been brought up and trained, with greater expense than you, my little ladies, could ever imagine or believe, to understand what a great artist I am. I could make them happy. When I did my very best I could make them perfectly happy." (Dinesen, 1953/1988:47,48)

Because Babette has prevailed in her own striving, her own problems of the heart in conflict with itself, she is able to offer up herself and her artistry as the medium through which the Brothers and Sisters gathered at her table engage and resolve their struggles, as well. While lost years are not retrieved for Martine and Philippa, General Loewenhielm and the elderly Brothers and Sisters, those years are blessed, and love, forgiveness, compassion, hope, and courage are the substance of the blessing. New joy is found, and laughter, play, and jubilation are retrieved. The years are not retrieved, but joy, blessedness, and happiness are.

> My life, I will not let you go except you bless me, but then I will let you go.

General Loewenhielm is able to let Martine go at last. The aged Brothers and Sisters are able to let go the long years of their lives. And Babette herself has been able to release Paris, the life she had enjoyed among her admirers, and her son and husband. Unlike the old woman in Dinesen's anecdote who would have liked to live her life over again, these characters do not need to live their lives over again so that they can know that they had them. Life has been hard, tragic even, but it has blessed them. In their own way, they have striven with God and humans and prevailed, and in so doing, they have, like Jacob, seen God's face.

Examining the Biblical Narratives

Let us attend closely now to certain of the biblical characters and stories within the frame of which we interpret further Dinesen's narratives and Faulkner's observations about humankind. First, the story of Cain. The narrative is brief, and it will be helpful to read it before launching into our analysis:

> Now Abel was a keeper of sheep, and Cain a tiller of the ground. In the course of time Cain brought to the Lord an offering of the fruit of the ground, and Abel for his part brought of the firstlings of his flock, their fat portions. And the Lord had regard for Abel and his offering, but for Cain and his offering he had no regard. So Cain was very angry, and his countenance fell. The Lord said to Cain, "Why are you angry, and why has your countenance fallen? If you do well, will you not be accepted? And if you do not do well, sin is lurking at the door; its desire is for you, but you must master it."
>
> Cain said to his brother Abel, "Let us go out to the field." And when they were in the field, Cain rose up against his brother Abel, and killed him. Then the Lord said to Cain, "Where is your brother Abel? He said, "I do not know; am I my brother's keeper?" And the Lord said, "What have you done? Listen; your brother's blood is crying out to me from the ground! And now you are cursed from the ground, which has opened its mouth to receive strength; you will be a fugitive and a wanderer on the earth." Cain said to the Lord, "My punishment is greater than I can bear! Today you have driven me away from the soil, and I shall be hidden from your face; I shall be a fugitive and a wanderer on the earth, and anyone who meets me may kill me." Then the Lord said to him, "Not so! Whoever kills Cain will suffer

a sevenfold vengeance." And the Lord put a mark on Cain, so that no one who came upon him would kill him. Then Cain went away from the presence of the Lord and settled in the Land of Nod, east of Eden. (Genesis 4:2b-16)

Cain's conflict is with the envy in his heart toward his brother Abel. The importance of the nature of his offering as compared to Abel's pales before the temptation posed by his envy and the rancorous feelings toward Abel which it evokes. God warns Cain that he must wrestle with this "dark angel": "Its desire is for you, but you must master it." Cain seems not to hear the promise couched in God's admonition. It is possible for him to master the angel. Instead, Cain lurches onward toward mortal confrontation with his brother. Just as he has not heard the implied promise in God's words, Cain also has not heard the dread foreboding, "its desire is for you." With alacrity, it seems, Cain strikes his brother down. Immediately, the narrative suggests, God asks, "Where is your brother Abel?" Here, Cain is offered a second chance to strive with the evil in his heart. He can open himself to remorse for his murderous sin against his brother, and thereby to repentance and mastery over the forces that desire him, *or* he can refuse again to strive with his dark angel. He chooses the latter and flings back an insolent retort, "I do not know; am I my brother's keeper?" A third time, God offers Cain the chance to strive and prevail: "What have you done? Listen; your brother's blood is crying out to me from the ground! And now you are cursed from the ground, which has opened its mouth to receive your brother's blood from your hand. When you till the ground, it will no longer yield to you its strength; you will be a fugitive and a wanderer on the earth." Cain can respond to God's piercing imagery, "Listen; your brother's blood is crying out to me from the ground!" and reverse his decline into self-annihilation, but he does not. Again, there is no attitude of regret for his brother's violent death, only fear of his own punishment and exile. Cain has repeatedly spurned God's proddings toward restoration and life and has chosen death instead, his brother's and his own. Because he has closed himself off from pity for his slain brother, he has forfeited the blessing which he might still have wrestled from his conflict. Instead of repentant acceptance of responsibility for his deed, Cain blames God for his sorry state: "Today you have driven me away from the soil, and I shall be hidden from your face; I shall be a fugitive and a wanderer on the earth, and anyone who meets me may kill me." Incredibly, Cain misses it *one more time*; a *fourth* time God offers Cain the chance to respond to God's loving persuasion: "'Not so! Whoever kills Cain will suffer a sevenfold vengeance.' And the Lord put a mark on Cain, so that no one who came upon him would kill him." Cain misses the suffering love in God's words and deed. We might imagine that by now Cain would prostrate himself before God in abject remorse for his terrible crime, but he does not. Having chosen not to struggle with the evil in his heart, he removes himself from God's presence; there will be no seeing God face to face, no blessing and new name: "Then Cain went away from the presence of the Lord, and settled in the land of Nod, east of Eden."

Cain's story has been for centuries the paradigmatic story of humankind's primeval strife of brother against brother. Storytellers of every era have told the story afresh. It continues to haunt us with its truth, because we see in it our own hates and our love affairs with those hates. John Steinbeck's twentieth century interpretation of the Cain and Abel story, *East of Eden*, beams contemporary light on the myriad ways we find to kill our brother and sister and resist the struggle to own our sin. Self-righteousness, injustice, intolerance, greed, prejudice, and war, Steinbeck reveals, assume newly sinister shapes in the present century, all coalescing to fortify humankind with new resistance to God's challenging question, "Where is your brother Abel?"

Let us turn now to the story which gave to Isak Dinesen her guiding image, personally and literarily, the story of Jacob's striving with the angel at Peniel. As this narrative also is quite short, let us read it thoughtfully:

> The same night he got up and took his two wives, his two maids, and his eleven children, and crossed the ford of the Jabbok. He took them and sent them across the stream, and likewise everything that he had. Jacob was left alone; and a man wrestled with him until daybreak. When the man saw that he did not prevail against Jacob, he struck him on the hip socket; and Jacob's hip was put out of joint as he wrestled with him. Then he said, "Let me go, for the day is breaking." But Jacob said, "I will not let you go, unless you bless me." So he said to him, "What is your name?" And he said, "Jacob." Then the man said, "You shall no longer be called Jacob, but Israel,

for you have striven with God and with humans, and have prevailed." Then Jacob asked him, "Please tell me your name." But he said, "Why is it that you ask my name?" And there he blessed him. So Jacob called the place Peniel, saying, "For I have seen God face to face, and yet my life is preserved." (Genesis 32:22–30)

Jacob's struggle needs to be examined in the context of what the morrow betides for him. He has learned that Esau is coming to meet him with four hundred men. Welcoming parties are not usually so generously constituted and, in light of Jacob's history with his brother, he has cause enough to worry. Having years ago cheated Esau of his birthright and their father Isaac's blessing, Jacob can expect Esau to be eager for revenge. Traveling back to his kindred with his wives, maids, and children, Jacob knows that he cannot simply show up on the doorstep as though his unmeritorious history with Esau had not happened. He sends ahead a present to his brother of "two hundred female goats and twenty male goats, two hundred ewes and twenty rams, thirty milk camels and their colts, forty cows and ten bulls, twenty female donkeys and ten male donkeys." (Genesis 32:14,15) Jacob thinks, "I may appease him with the present that goes ahead of me, and afterwards I shall see his face; perhaps he will accept me" (Genesis 32:20b).

It is at this point that the story of the struggle at Peniel begins. We can understand that Jacob is having trouble sleeping. He sends his family and retinue across the stream and remains alone to wrestle with the angel. There is a lot to wrestle with, but unlike Cain who refuses to do so, Jacob wrestles mightily throughout the night. Furthermore, Jacob had already engaged his battle the preceding day with his decision to send his gifts ahead to Esau and to implore acceptance. With the breaking of day, Jacob struggles on, refusing to disengage the conflict within his heart, "unless you bless me." Finally, Jacob wins the blessing but not before a dear price is exacted: "When the man saw that he did not prevail against Jacob, he struck him on the hip socket; and Jacob's hip was put out of joint as he wrestled with him." As "the one who strives with God," Jacob wins a new name, Israel, "for you have striven with God and with humans, and have prevailed." Having received a new name, Jacob gives a name. He calls the place of his struggle Peniel, "For I have seen God face to face, and yet my life is preserved."

Before reflecting on the meaning of Peniel, Jacob's claim to have seen "the face of God," let us give a little more attention to his earlier decision to send gifts of goats, camels, cows, and donkeys to Esau. Was Jacob faking it one more time? Was this just a ploy to save his own hide? Or did Jacob sincerely repent of his treacherous dealings with his brother even before this night of striving beside the Jabbok? If not, have the night's strivings resolved any lingering conflict in Jacob's heart concerning his relationship with his brother and what he needs now to do? For help with answering our questions, let us continue reading the story as it develops the next day:

> Now Jacob looked up and saw Esau coming, and four hundred men with him. So he divided the children among Leah and Rachel and the two maids. He put the maids with their children in front, then Leah with her children, and Rachel and Joseph last of all. He himself went on ahead of them, bowing himself to the ground seven times, until he came near his brother.
>
> But Esau ran to meet him, and embraced him, and fell on his neck and kissed him, and they wept. When Esau looked up and saw the women and children, he said, "Who are these with you?" Jacob said, "The children whom God has graciously given *your servant*." Then the maids drew near, they and their children, and bowed down; Leah likewise and her children drew near and bowed down; and finally Joseph and Rachel drew near, and they bowed down. Esau said, "What do you mean by all this company that I met?" Jacob answered, *"To find favor with my Lord."* But Esau said, "I have enough, my brother; keep what you have for yourself." Jacob said, "No, please; if I find favor with you, then accept my present from my hand; for *truly to see your face is like seeing the face of God*—since you have received me with such favor. Please accept my gift that is brought to you, because God has dealt graciously with me, and because I have everything I want." So he urged him and he took it. (Genesis 33:1–11, emphasis added)

Jacob's repentance is contrite and genuine. The struggle beside the Jabbok through a long, exhausting, and perilous night has been an experience of redemption, a seeing God face to face. Jacob is now Israel. Now he feels compassion for the brother he had deceived and swindled and repentance for his sin against him. Now he has courage to meet his brother and hope that they can be reconciled. Now he can relate to Esau with integrity and honor; he can love his brother again. Instead of conniving to usurp his older brother's position, Jacob is willing to be his brother's servant. Now, Jacob can say to the twin brother from whom he has been so long estranged, " . . . truly to see your face is like seeing the face of God."

Though the Yahwist does not show it to us, we can surmise that Esau has at some point had his own dark night of struggle, and he, too, has prevailed, because he shows to Jacob a God-like face! " . . . you have received me with such favor." Jacob is overwhelmed by his brother's generosity of spirit and affectionate forgiveness. "But Esau ran to meet him, and embraced him, and they wept."

Lest I paint a picture which is too idyllic, however, I need to acknowledge that Jacob as Israel is not discontinuous with Jacob as Jacob. He is not miraculously now an altogether different person. The transformed Jacob is still thoroughly human and subject to human limitations and foibles. Thus, he prepares himself for the worst with Esau and approaches him with suspicion and calculation. Arranging his company so that the ones he values most will be the last encountered by Esau and his men, and thus most likely to escape an assault, Jacob positions Zilpah and Bilhah and their children ahead of Leah and her children, and Rachel and Joseph he places last. Stationing himself at the front, Jacob meets Esau, we can imagine, with eyes narrowed and darting. Most revealing, perhaps, is Jacob's continuing mistrust of his brother and inability to accept his offer to leave several men for his assistance, despite Esau's extravagant and forgiving reception of him. As Gerhard von Rad points out: "One sees . . . how little confidence Jacob has in this turn of affairs for the good by his stubborn refusal of Esau's friendly offer to accompany him. That is the mistrust of one who himself has often deceived" (von Rad, 1961:328). As Jacob has been permanently left with a physical limp, his life story, flawed by deceit and trickery, has left him with a psychic limp, as well. Jacob's life has been blessed, but he bears permanently the marks of its distortions.

It is not surprising that Isak Dinesen took this story as her life paradigm when we realize its enormous power to capture an entire nation's imagination in like manner. Von Rad points out that Jacob's struggle and consequent limp became the nation Israel's image for its own history of striving with God. Consequently, the cultic ritual of sacrifice became one which included severing the sciatic nerve of the sacrificial animal. Both Jacob now Israel and the nation bearing his name, von Rad observes, "emerged from this struggle broken" (von Rad, 1961:323).

I think that *this holding together of brokenness and blessing* lies at the heart of Israel's intuition, and Dinesen's as well. It accepts the reality of life's harshness while refusing to despair and split reality into dualistic, dichotomous poles. Indeed, *the very possibility of seeing God's face is wed to conflict and brokenness that are, at once, context and result of struggle.*

We recall that Cain refused to struggle and absented himself from God's presence. Jacob, on the other hand, accepts the struggle and refuses to turn loose until it is finished. He holds on, knowing that he cannot coerce happiness or victory from the striving; what he does sense is that he can come to a place of truth and integrity, though not without cost. These, truth and integrity, are his blessing and the aspect of the face of God itself. Jacob learns that life lived in God's presence bears the nature of truth-telling. Cain refused to learn this healing reality though God repeatedly held out its prospect to him.

Jacob's gift of goats, camels, and rams to Esau prefigures the restoration to hospitable life together in a unified house which is now opening up for the estranged brothers. It prefigures as well the divine-human narrative of hospitality which will be completed in the life, death, and resurrection of Jesus of Nazareth.

More than Cain or Jacob, David is a character of great complexity and uncommon gifts. His story exhibits humanity's struggle with the dark angel on a scale grand enough to incorporate lesser figures like Cain and the elderly Brothers and Sisters of Berlevaag and greater stories of greater figures like Jacob and Babette. Israel's king, David sinks into the stork's talons and struggles there for ascension from the death he has imposed on himself and his house. Like Jacob's, his victory will be extracted from the crucible of brokenness and blessing.

As we move to David's story, we find congruent strains with both the Cain story and the Jacob story. Though it is lengthy, let us read the narrative thoughtfully and closely again:

96

In the spring of the year, the time when kings go out to battle, David sent Joab with his officers and all Israel with him; they ravaged the Ammonites, and besieged Rabbah. But David remained at Jerusalem.

It happened, late one afternoon, when David rose from his couch and was walking about on the roof of the king's house, that he saw from the roof a woman bathing; the woman was very beautiful. David sent someone to inquire about the woman. It was reported, "This is Bathsheba, daughter of Eliam, the wife of Uriah the Hittite." So David sent messengers to get her, and she came to him, and he lay with her. (Now she was purifying herself after her period). Then she returned to her house. The woman conceived; and she sent and told David, "I am pregnant."

So David sent word to Joab, "Send me Uriah the Hittite." And Joab sent Uriah to David. When Uriah came to him, David asked how Joab and the people fared, and how the war was going. Then David said to Uriah, "Go down to your house, and wash your feet." Uriah went out of the king's house, and there followed him a present from the king. But Uriah slept at the entrance of the king's house with all the servants of his lord, and did not go down to his house. When they told David, "Uriah did not go down to his house," David said to Uriah, "You have just come from a journey. Why did you not go down to your house?" Uriah said to David, "The ark and Israel and Judah remain in booths; and my lord Joab and the servants of my lord are camping in the open field; shall I then go to my house, to eat and to drink, and to lie with my wife? As you live, and as your soul lives, I will not do such a thing." Then David said to Uriah, "Remain here today also, and tomorrow I will send you back." On the next day, David invited him to eat and drink in his presence and made him drunk; and in the evening he went out to lie on his couch with the servants of his lord, but he did not go down to his house.

In the morning David wrote a letter to Joab, and sent it by the hand of Uriah. In the letter he wrote, "Set Uriah in the forefront of the hardest fighting, and then draw back from him, so that he may be struck down and die." As Joab was besieging the city, he assigned Uriah to the place where he knew there were valiant warriors. The men of the city came out and fought with Joab; and some of the servants of David among the people fell. Uriah the Hittite was killed as well. . . .

When the wife of Uriah heard that her husband was dead, she made lamentation for him. When the mourning was over, David sent and brought her to his house, and she became his wife, and bore him a son.

But the thing that David had done displeased the Lord, and the Lord sent Nathan to David. He came to him, and said to him, "There were two men in a certain city, the one rich and the other poor. The rich man had very many flocks and herds; but the poor man had nothing but one little ewe lamb, which he had bought. He brought it up, and it grew up with him and with his children; it used to eat of his meager fare, and drink from his cup, and lie in his bosom, and it was like a daughter to him. Now there came a traveler to the rich man, and he was loath to take one of his own flock or herd to prepare for the wayfarer who had come to him, but he took the poor man's lamb, and prepared that for the guest who had come to him." Then David's anger was greatly kindled against the man. He said to Nathan, "As the Lord lives, the man who has done this deserves to die; he shall restore the lamb fourfold, because he did this thing, and because he had no pity."

Nathan said to David, "You are the man! Thus says the Lord, the God of Israel: I anointed you king over Israel, and I rescued you from the hand of Saul; I gave you your master's house, and your master's wives into your bosom, and gave you the house of Israel and of Judah; and if that had been too little, I would have added as much more. Why have you despised the word of the Lord, to do what is evil in his sight? You have struck down Uriah the Hittite with the sword, and have taken his wife to be your wife, and have killed him with the sword of the Ammonites. Now therefore the sword shall never depart from your house, for you have despised me and have taken the wife of Uriah the Hittite to be your wife. Thus says the Lord: I will raise up trouble against you from within your own house; and I will take your wives before your eyes, and give them to your neighbor, and he shall lie with your wives in the sight of this very sun. For you did it secretly; but I will do this thing before all Israel, and before the sun." David said to Nathan, "I have sinned against the Lord." Nathan said to David, "Now the Lord has put away your sin; you shall not die. Nevertheless, because by this deed you have utterly scorned the lord, the child that is born to you shall die." Then Nathan went to his house. (2 Samuel 11:1–17,26,27; 12:1–15a)

Like Cain, David has murdered. Like Jacob, he has practiced deceit and manipulation. David, however, is a rather more complex character than Jacob and significantly more complex than Cain. David's life story is, thus, also more complex, fraught with ambiguities, contradictions, and profundities. He is exceedingly intelligent but capable of stupid actions. He is both sensitive and callous, reverent and idolatrous. A man after God's own heart, he despises his beloved. Understanding this brilliant and convoluted character is aided by the help of other brilliant minds like Faulkner's and Dinesen's.

Faulkner cautioned young writers not to fritter their talents away on stories of mere lust rather than love, or of "defeats in which nobody loses anything of value," or of "victories without hope and, worst of all, without pity or compassion" (Faulkner, in Cowley, ed., 1946/1987:724). Certainly, the ancient writer of the David story has not trivialized his talent in the way Faulkner warned against. While David's story with Bathsheba is one of lust, it is not a cheap romance novel titillation, but the struggle of a great heart with its own contradictions. David's story is one of lust *and* love, and who would deny that its defeats are those in which much of great value is lost? A man loses his life at the hand of enemy soldiers, a baby dies, and David's house is stabbed with tragedy for generations to come. But the David story is also a story of victory, a story of striving with the dark angel until the blessing is given; it is a story of descending into the stork's talons and ascending again, and thereby, it is a story of hope. Uriah's defeat and David's infamous victory over him are finally, through Nathan's redemptive intervention, transformed into a story of pity and compassion. "I have sinned against the Lord." David's terse, repentant confession is courageous and intelligent. As Carolyn Heilbrun says of Hamlet's mother, "If there is one quality that has characterized, and will characterize, every speech of [David's] in the [story], it is the ability to see reality clearly, and to express it. This talent is not lost when turned upon [himself]" (Heilbrun, 1990:16).

David's unwitting self-denunciation prior to Nathan's identification of him as the guilty man pinpoints the heart of the murderer's sin, " . . . because he had no pity." Cain, we have seen, neither expressed nor felt pity for his brother Abel whom he had cut down. David, however, accepts his guilt and, far from blaming God for his downfall as Cain had done, receives Nathan's story as his own. His angry and passionate pity for the victimized man becomes remorse for his own actions and pity for Uriah. We can speculate that David's struggle with his heart over his sin had already begun even before Nathan requested audience with him.

Like Jacob, he has already known sleepless nights. David knows that he has acted without pity and achieved a sorry victory over Uriah, resulting in a defeat that, for Uriah, has been an ultimate one. But Nathan's call to repentance pierces David's heart and awakens compassion which allows him now to engage his struggle fully. Like Jacob again, David stands in the darkness, trembling beside the Jabbok; like Dinesen, he is about to descend into "the tight place," the dark pit of the stork's talon. But he does not shrink back in impudent cowardice with the surliness of Cain's ignoble retort: "Am I my brother's keeper?" He stands with face bared to God and hears the words of God through Nathan:

> You are the man! Thus says the Lord, the God of Israel: I anointed you king over Israel, and I rescued you from the hand of Saul; I gave you your master's house, and your master's wives into your bosom, and gave you the house of Israel and of Judah; and if that had been too little, I would have added as much more. Why have you despised the word of the Lord, to do what is evil in his sight? You have struck down Uriah the Hittite with the sword, and have taken his wife to be your wife, and have killed him with the sword of the Ammonites. Now therefore the sword shall never depart from your house, for you have despised me, and have taken the wife of Uriah the Hittite to be your wife. Thus says the Lord; I will raise up trouble against you from within your own house; and I will take your wives before your very eyes, and give them to your neighbor, and he shall lie with your wives in the sight of this very sun. For you did it secretly; but I will do this thing before all Israel, and before the sun. (2 Samuel 12:7–12)

With God's sentence, David's night of wrestling begins in force. He has engaged the problems of his heart in its self-conflict by admitting his sin; still, he must lie in the pit of his making. Because he has felt pity and has repented, he will not die, but long years of struggle in the tight places of the stork's talons will leave him stricken; like Jacob, he will henceforth walk with the limp of his treachery.

But like Jacob, too, he will emerge blessed. As with Babette, so too will David sacrifice his genius for Israel and for God. Bearing full, courageous responsibility for the unavoidable consequences of his sins, David will strive with his own heart, with God, and with humans, and he will prevail through living out his God-given purpose despite numerous falls into the stork's talons. In his own way, he will descend into hell and rise again. At the end, if not David himself, others for millenia will see the stork's image. David will wrest the blessing from his striving and to him a new name will be given. Jesus himself will be called Son of David.

Other characters in the Hebrew Bible struggle with their conflicted hearts, experiencing fall and redemption, death and resurrection; some, like Babette and David, are persons of great talent; others are persons of commonplace abilities striving with hardships which, though commonplace, are also exacting. Esther is an example of the former; Tamar, the latter.

Esther's struggle is not with a sin committed but with the temptation to escape injury, perhaps death, by refusing to stand forward in defense of others. Appealed to by Mordecai to use her queenly influence to save the Jews who, through Haman's machinations have been condemned to die, Esther does an interesting tap dance in an attempt to sidestep the issue. She delays a struggle with her heart which, doubtless, she knows she will not be able to evade for long.

Esther helps us understand our anthropology. We know her feelings. She wants it all simply to go away, and hence she tries to ignore the magnitude of the problem. Evidently, though the storyteller is less than clear at this point, Esther's maids and eunuchs do not at first tell her why Mordecai has clothed himself in sackcloth and ashes and is standing wailing at the king's gate. The aspect of her uncle displaying himself in this way distresses Esther, even deeply, the narrativist tells us, but she curiously tries to treat the symptoms without inquiring about their cause. Has she heard rumors? Perhaps one of her maids has told her something. In any case, her first response is to send clothing to Mordecai and request him to take off the sackcloth and clean himself up; the tap dance has begun. Mordecai, however, is in no mood to dance. He refuses Esther's offer. Next, Esther sends Hathach outside to ask Mordecai what all this means. We can guess that she is hoping things are not as bad as they seem. When Hathach returns with a copy of Ahasuerus' decree mandating the death of the Jews and Mordecai's plea that she appeal to the king in her people's behalf, Esther's struggle begins in earnest. Dancing cannot make it all go away. Esther knows that she occupies a unique and powerful position. She also knows that the king loves her deeply. If anyone can sway him from this course, she can. But she has a secret, one that Mordecai helped her concoct. Like Jacob, she has not always played fair and gained her position without deceit. Ahasuerus does not know she is a Jew. Esther is afraid to tell him; will he be incensed by her failure to be truthful about her lineage? Will he include her among the Jews to be executed? Esther's struggle with her heart is as intense as Jacob's beside the Jabbok and David's in the palace throne room.

She tries once more to deflect Mordecai's appeal. Sending Hathach back to her obstinate kinsman, she sends a message about her own position of peril. Esther reminds him that everyone knows that not even the queen is permitted to approach the king in the inner court unless summoned. To do so without being called is to incur the sentence of death. By extending his golden scepter to the intruder, the king can annul the sentence, but Esther suggests she cannot count on his doing that. Because he has not called her in a month, she suggests, things are not going all that great for them right now.

Mordecai will not be put off, however. He knows that Esther is tapping as fast as she can, and we can imagine that he feels compassion for her in her predicament. Still, she is the Jews' only hope. First, Mordecai strikes fear into her heart, manipulation not being beneath him; finally, to Mordecai's credit, he challenges her to rise to greatness. He has pulled out all the stops. Esther has, no doubt, paced the royal bedroom sleepless with her own nocturnal struggle with the dark angel. She decides. On the side of courage, integrity, pity, justice, and love for her people Esther decides. And she decides to act from within the strengthening setting of the community of the faithful who will fast and pray with her. "Go, gather all the Jews to be found in Susa, and hold a fast on my behalf, and neither eat nor drink for three days, night or day. After that I will go to the king, though it is against the law, and if I perish I perish." (Esther 4:16)

Esther exercises her own decision-making power and steps out of the mold. She is more than Ahasuerus' beautiful and prized wife. She is queen and responsible for exercising her authority and influence on behalf of her condemned people. She is a compassionate and courageous human being willing to risk her life for a true story and a life story truly lived. Her struggle has been difficult, and she has flirted with cowardice and self-protection before everything else. We are familiar with both the feelings and the deeds. But from the center of the fasting, worshiping community supporting her, she is enabled to respond to Mordecai's challenge: "Who knows? Perhaps you have come to royal dignity for just such a time as this" (Esther 4:14b).

Intelligent, complex, convoluted, Esther's character, like David's, is capable of greatness and tragedy. Like David's life story, Esther's is marred by deception and self-serving choices and actions. Like David too, Esther extracts her soul from the struggle within her conflicted heart. Her fall into the dark pit of her making and her subsequent wrestle with the dark angel are redemptively faced, and blessing is won from brokenness. Her courageous struggle and victory save the lives of her people and redeem her own from its truthlessness. By repairing her own integrity and opening the House of Israel to God's purposes and hospitality, Esther defeats Haman's efforts to impose evil and death. The image of God in Esther shines forth through her valiant struggle and its transformative resolution; we can say that Esther, too, has seen the face of God.

A female character in scripture very different from Esther, but sharing attributes of intelligence, resolve, and courage with her, is Tamar, daughter-in-law of Judah. Like Esther's, Tamar's struggle is an ambiguous and conflicted one with survival on the line. Although again we will not look directly at the text, I point the reader to the biblical narrative in order to get the story in hand; it is found in Genesis 38.

Tamar's struggle for the blessing contains elements of ambiguity and overarching grace which we have come to recognize and expect from their presence in other biblical narratives. As with Jacob, David, and Esther, deceit is mixed with courage in Tamar's character. Divine grace at last reveals the stork's image; Tamar's offspring is a forebear of Jesus. But let us follow the story and reconstruct Tamar's struggle with her own heart, God, and others. If, like Jacob, she is to see God's face and prevail, she must also, like Jacob, engage and endure the long night's struggle.

Tamar's narrative begins hopefully. She is wed to Judah's firstborn, Er. As wife of a landowner, her economic and social future is secure. But Er is wicked, and God cuts his life short. Judah gives his second son Onan to Tamar, but Onan also dies because of his rebellion against God, and Tamar is left widowed and childless. Judah's youngest son Shelah is still a boy, so Tamar is sent back to her father's house with the promise of marriage to Shelah when he is of age.

The years pass and Shelah is an eligible young bachelor, but no action is forthcoming from Judah to fulfill his promise to Tamar. Now she is faced with advancing years when her child-bearing ability will be past and there will be no means of insuring her survival without husband or sons. What can she do? We can imagine the play of fear and anger in Tamar's heart. Judah has not kept his word to her. Her very existence is at stake. Her careful, studied deception is a desperate gamble. If it does not work, she can be put to death for harlotry.

Fully aware of the risk she is taking, after her mother-in-law's death, Tamar disguises herself as a temple prostitute and entices Judah into her bed. In payment, Judah promises her a kid from his flock for which he leaves behind his signet, cord, and staff as pledge. When her pregnancy is discovered and Judah orders that she be burned for whoredom, Tamar produces the identifying artifacts and with them proof of Judah's patrimony. To Judah's credit, he acknowledges his responsibility and even goes so far as to concede that Tamar has acted with more integrity than he, since he had reneged on his early promise to her. Tamar's twins are born, and Perez, son of Judah and Tamar, is listed in Matthew's genealogy of Jesus.

Alone and growing old without children, Tamar found herself in the dark pit of the stork's talon. But like other strugglers before and since, she wrestled with her dark angel and prevailed. In so doing, she became an ancestor of Jesus the Messiah with her name inscribed in the Matthean genealogy, one of only a few women named in that list.

Because Tamar is not the great character Esther is, with responsibilities impinging on the welfare of the entire nation, her narrative seems at once both more and less interesting than Esther's. She is more like us. Her personal struggle, although hardly significant for an entire people, is no less intense, no less dramatic and mortal.

Tamar's story recapitulates the universal human drama of birth, death, and resurrection, and prefigures the Judeo-Christian vision of creation, fall, and redemption. That her son Perez is an ancestor of Jesus completes her narrative as prototype of God's story with humankind. Tamar is a fallen and resurrected creature of God whose struggle with the dark angel extracts blessing from brokenness, participating finally in God's own miracle of incarnation and transformation in Jesus Christ. Like all before and after her, Tamar's narrative is one of struggle and journey into the house of God, where face to face companionship with God and others is enjoyed and celebrated. By traversing that journey and engaging that struggle, Tamar unfolds the plot of her life story as one created *imago Dei*, in the image of God.

It seems curious that Mary the mother of Jesus has often received less attention than other female characters in scripture. As one struggling with the dark angel and her conflicted heart, however, Mary can hardly have waged a lesser struggle than those characters we have already examined. Perhaps the evangelists' portrayals of Mary are partly responsible for this seeming neglect; there she appears passive, indistinct, and not fully drawn literarily. Still, careful attention to what the authors *have* given us can yield a picture not unlike those we have already seen.

> In the sixth month the angel Gabriel was sent from God to a city of Galilee named Nazareth, to a virgin betrothed to a man whose name was Joseph, of the house of David; and the virgin's name was Mary. And he came to her and said, "Hail, O favored one, the Lord is with you!" But she was greatly troubled at the saying, and considered in her mind what sort of greeting this might be. And the angel said to her, "Do not be afraid, Mary, for you have found favor with God. And behold, you will conceive in your womb and bear a son, and you shall call his name Jesus. He will be great, and will be called the Son of the Most High; and the Lord God will give to him the throne of his father David, and he will reign over the house of Jacob for ever; and of his kingdom there will be no end." And Mary said to the angel, "How can this be, since I have no husband?" And the angel said to her, "The Holy Spirit will come upon you, And the power of the Most High will overshadow you; therefore the child to be born will be called holy, the son of God. And behold, your kinswoman Elizabeth in her old age has also conceived a son; and this is the sixth month with her who was called barren. For with God nothing will be impossible." And Mary said, "Behold, I am the handmaid of the Lord; let it be to me according to your word." (Luke 1:26–38a, RSV)

Engaged to Joseph, Mary is shocked to discover that she will bear a son who is not Joseph's. What will others say? Will they call for her stoning? What will be Joseph's response? How should she appropriate this news? Luke's brief narrative gives us only the barest look at Mary's struggle. But who can doubt its reality and its fearful dimensions? Mary undergoes her own struggle with the angel; in this instance, the angel has a name: Gabriel. It is fitting that Gabriel seeks to allay her fear, for his message is fearful. To be with child and not yet married was in Mary's day—and has not ceased to be in this day—a fearful situation for a young woman. We can surmise that Mary's struggle to understand and to extract a blessing from this unexpected predicament lasts longer than the few moments Luke's narrative might lead his readers to think. It could well be that her lengthy, subsequent visit to her cousin Elizabeth concerns just that struggle to come to terms with her predicament. In any case, like others in similar struggles, Mary emerges with a clearer view of God's face and a more finely etched definition of herself: "Here am I, the servant of the Lord; let it be with me according to your word." Though Luke has her speaking these words right away in response to the angel, it is likely that the assent of her mind and heart to her words comes at the end of her own long night beside the Jabbok. From this point onward, Mary's story will continue to be one unfolded through many descents into the stork's talons, with her vigil at the cross the deepest and darkest of all. But the blessing comes after the brokenness for Mary, as for other strugglers of faith. Her son is the Christ of all Christendom.

As mother of Jesus, Mary's role in God's drama and adventure with humankind is more than we can fully unfold. To be sure, her parenting of the infant and boy Jesus can hardly be diminished; for good or ill, we know the enormous influence practically all mothers have on their children. Beginning her struggle before Jesus' birth and continuing it through the years moving toward the cross, Mary surely re-enacts the divine-human drama we now identify clearly. By living it faithfully, Mary images God through Jesus' years of growing up and expresses her own essential identity as one created *imago Dei*. Haltingly, but faithfully, Mary is struggler, face to face companion of God, mother of Jesus and partner with God in humankind's redemptive transformation and consummation.

The Human Struggles of Jesus

As we come to Jesus himself, we need to pose a question: If our anthropological examination is of "the human heart in conflict with itself," can Jesus be our central character here, as he is the central figure in humanity's redemption? Did he, too, struggle with himself, God, and others and, in so doing, come face to face with God? Was *his* blessing extracted from the crucible of brokenness as well? The biblical narratives offer affirmative answers to all these queries. Let us follow important ones of those stories to assess my claim. First, the temptation in the wilderness.

> And Jesus, full of the Holy Spirit, returned from the Jordan, and was led by the Spirit for forty days in the wilderness, tempted by the devil. And he ate nothing in those days; and when they were ended, he was hungry. The devil said to him, "If you are the Son of God, command this stone to become bread." And Jesus answered him, "It is written, 'Man shall not live by bread alone.'"
> And the devil took him up, and showed him all the kingdoms of the world in a moment of time, and said to him, "To you I will give all this authority and their glory; for it has been delivered to me, and I give it to whom I will. If you, then, will worship me, it shall all be yours." And Jesus answered him, "It is written,
> 'You shall worship the Lord your God,
>   and him only shall you serve.'"
> And he took him to Jerusalem, and set him on the pinnacle of the temple, and said to him, "If you are the Son of God, throw yourself down from here; for it is written,
> 'He will give his angels charge of you,
>   to guard you,'
> and
> 'On their hands they will bear you up,
>   lest you strike your foot against a stone.'"
> And Jesus answered him, "It is said, 'You shall not tempt the Lord your God.'" And when the devil had ended every temptation, he departed from him until an opportune time. (Luke 4:1–13, RSV)

Most of the preaching and Christian education I experienced as a young Baptist growing up suggested that Jesus turned aside Satan's tempting offers with never a pause and the whole episode lasted a mere few minutes, despite the fact that we are told the wilderness sojourn was of forty days duration. That docetic view was consistent with the tacitly accepted notion that a divine Jesus was not *really* a human being who could desire power, acclaim, or even food. The wilderness thing was pretty much a staged deal to show Satan who was boss. Eastern North Carolina Baptist faith was in a Jesus who rode over the heads of all the rest of us human weaklings so susceptible to the tricky ways of the devil. Jesus as our model for anthropology, the human who would cut a way through the forest for us, got lost in the docetism. We knew little, if anything, of the carpenter from Nazareth who had his own problems with a conflicted heart.

Whatever one might think of *The Last Temptation of Christ*, the movie which evoked such a storm of controversy a few years ago, the film challenged viewers to deal with the possibility that Jesus, like us, was torn by conflict and struggled throughout his ministry with opposing enticements. Likewise, the drama *Jesus Christ Superstar* raised similar issues in the seventies. Are these contemporary treatments of the Christ theme in any way on target? If so, to what degree? *Did* Jesus, like the rest of us, waver between cowardice and courage, between insensitivity—perhaps even brutality—on the one hand, and compassion, on the other; between self-aggrandizement and self-sacrifice? Could it be that only such a thoroughly human Jesus can really unlock our prisons and free us? Did Jesus also struggle to live a truthful story, the story of life in God's house, trustworthy companion to God and all others? If he did, perhaps our own struggles to live stories of truth and reliable companionship can be engaged with less debilitating guilt and more hope.

With those hypothetical questions and suppositions before us, let us look more closely at the story of the wilderness temptation. It is immediately after his baptism, just when Jesus is full of the Spirit of God, that he is tempted. The significance of this juxtaposition should not escape us;. it suggests at least two things. First, there is never a time when, safe within our spirituality, we are immune to temptation and struggle. Second, struggle is not all bad; rather, it is a time when we engage issues and perhaps settle some things, at least for a time. The forty days duration of Jesus' wilderness experience and the fact that he did not eat during that time demonstrate the intense wrestling which he underwent. More than Jacob, Jesus wrestles a powerful adversary, the darkest of angels. And his struggle lasts more than a night. But like Jacob, Jesus refuses to disengage the conflict until he has been blessed. Like Jacob, too, he will emerge changed, in some way wounded, foreshadowing the Gethsemane struggle and the Calvary crucifixion. Having conquered the dark forces within his heart which would seduce him from his course and confuse his identity, Jesus enjoys a respite, although not a long one. Luke tells us that Satan left him "until an opportune time." Jesus has descended into the stork's talons and ascended again. But there will be other plunges into dark pits of temptation and inner conflict and other ascents to faithfulness.

Does this story revealingly interlace with our own personal stories of fragile and groping experience? Does Jesus' struggle reveal something about ours, giving us hope that we will prevail through enabling grace and gift? After each penultimate death, will there also be for us a penultimate resurrection and new life? Will this be humankind's pattern until the last death and final resurrection?

Keeping these questions in focus, let us move forward to the Gethsemane story. Mark's narrative deserves close attention. Let us examine it step by step.

> They went to a place called Gethsemane; and he said to his disciples, "Sit here while I pray." (Mark 14:32)

This may well be the most forlorn of all the stories the evangelists give us. Surrounded by his closest friends, Jesus yet will find himself alone.

> He took with him Peter and James and John, and began to be distressed and agitated. (Mark 14:33)

The struggle has begun. What lies ahead will not be easy. Great suffering, Jesus knows, will be his lot if his story continues to unfold as he has lived it to this point.

> And he said to them, "I am deeply grieved, even to death; remain here, and keep awake." (Mark 14:34)

Mark lets his readers in on the depth of Jesus' struggle. His suffering distress is characterized as profound grief "even to death." The wilderness struggle was only the first act in a continuing drama which Jesus must now find the strength to live out, no matter the consequences. He implores Peter, James, and John to stay awake with him through the terrifying hours ahead.

> And going a little farther, he threw himself on the ground and prayed that, if it were possible, the hour might pass from him. (Mark 14:35)

The struggle now is fully engaged for Jesus. Like Jacob, his ordeal with his heart and with God takes place in the night with those who are dearest to him nearby. However, as with Jacob, too, Jesus finds that he wrestles alone. The intensity of his lonely struggle continues through the night.

> He said, "Abba, Father, for you all things are possible; remove this cup from me; yet, not what I want, but what you want." (Mark 14:36)

This is the climax of Jesus' struggle. Like all people, Jesus wishes to escape dreaded suffering, but he is committed to living through the darkness. Only so will the blessing come. Like Jacob asking the angel's name and refusing to disengage the combat unless he is blessed, Jesus will not push the cup away. Unless God wishes to remove it and does so, Jesus will drink it fully. He will emerge from the struggle halt but blessed.

Is Jesus' experience in any way like ours? Interlacing the Gethsemane story with the faith community's story at Watts Street Baptist Church again will illumine important aspects of our humanity. In a sermon entitled "How Can Christians Become Christian?" Mel Williams reflects on Matthew Fox's book *Creation Spirituality*. Mel observes that Fox enumerates four paths of spirituality, the second of which is "daring the dark." Mel comments:

> This is the path to God that moves through the struggles, the difficulties of life, the "dark night of the soul," as the mystics call it. It's the power we receive from facing the negatives in our life, the shadow part of our life, the parts of our life we may not like. When we reach the end of our rope, the edge of despair or apathy, we may try to cover up our anger or fear or pain. Part of our spiritual journey is facing the pain. Allowing ourselves to experience the pain, the grief. "When the heart is broken, then compassion can begin to flow through it." (Williams, 1991:3,4)

Adding another thread to our interlacing, I think it is fair to say that this is what the hymnist meant by "sanctified distress."

The beloved hymn "How Firm A Foundation" promises that even our deepest distress will be sanctified to us. Surely this is what Fox and Williams are talking about. And surely it is what Jesus experienced in Gethsemane and afterwards.

> He came and found them sleeping; and he said to Peter, "Simon, are you asleep? Could you not keep awake one hour? Keep awake and pray that you may not come into the time of trial; the spirit indeed is willing, but the flesh is weak." (Mark 14:37,38)

Jesus needs the community of those who care about him and believe in the story they and he are living together. His journey toward God's house has not at any point been taken in solitary isolation, and it has never been for himself alone. He appeals to his companions to watch and pray with him.

> And again he went away and prayed, saying the same words. And once more he came and found them sleeping, for their eyes were very heavy; and they did not know what to say to him. (Mark 14:39,40)

Lonely, frightened, fearing the coming morning's events, Jesus has only a sleeping band of friends to comfort him. It is too little, but Jesus nonetheless resolves his struggle. He has dared the dark. And like Israel who was Jacob, Jesus is empowered now to be fully who he is, the Son of Man.

> He came a third time and said to them, "Are you still sleeping and taking your rest? Enough! The hour has come; the Son of Man is betrayed into the hands of sinners. Get up, let us be going. See, my betrayer is at hand. (Mark 14:41,42)

As Son of Man, Child of Humanity, Jesus has descended into the stork's talons and ascended again. Living the human condition with us in all its disappointment, threat, and peril, Jesus has grappled with his fear and wish to protect himself and to shrink from his conflict. And he has prevailed, like Jacob, with God, himself, and others.

The Gethsemane story leads to the crucifixion. What Jesus has resolved in the struggle in the garden he completes on the cross. His burden still, however, is to understand and withstand the godforsakenness he feels at the terrible hour of death. Our purpose here is not to answer what numerous biblical scholars have only partly explained regarding the nature of the godforsakenness Jesus suffers. That mystery can be only dimly known. Rather, by attending to this last event in Jesus' struggle with the dark angel, we can look into the deepest depths of the pit and see that, even there, the struggle for the blessing can be waged and won. Jesus, our exemplar, is also our power; model and paradigm, he is more: he is our Redeemer.

> When it was noon, darkness came over the whole land until three in the afternoon. At three o'clock Jesus cried out with a loud voice, "Eloi, Eloi, lema sabachthani?" which means, "My God, my God, why have you forsaken me?" (Mark 15:33–34)

Jesus' struggle with the dark angel now reaches its climax. His agony is at its sharpest, close to unbearable. I recall Julie Harris' portrayal of Isak Dinesen's struggle with the searing spinal pain of advanced, terminal syphilis. The production of *Lucifer's Child* at Duke University was superb, and Harris' one-woman enactment splendid. Writhing on the floor, flat on her back, Harris in the role of Dinesen showed this courageous woman's refusal to submit to the dark angel. Indeed, she grappled with her adversary and demanded that it bless her. In all her pain, Dinesen knew that *it* must not speak the last word. It must not claim her soul. She would ascend out of the stork's talon, even as she had escaped that dark pit so many times before.

Like Jacob and Dinesen, Jesus prevails in his struggle and is given a new name—"wonderful counselor, almighty God, Prince of Peace." The struggle has opened the doors to God's world house and otherworld house. Now, those who stood fearful without are welcomed inside; those who were rejected and despised are extended God's hospitality in Jesus the Christ. It is to resurrection and hospitality that the plot of Jesus' story now leads.

Narrative Anthropology: Theology, Humanity, and Story

The scholarly theological work of interlacing the biblical passion narrative with our ecclesial story, Dinesen's *Babette's Feast*, and our communal and personal narratives serves the church's work of shaping a Christian doctrine of humankind. Such a narrative methodology affords an approach to the systematic task of identifying, interpreting, and, in a measure, transforming the doctrine of humanity and its constituting components. Central to this labor is the task of analyzing anew the doctrine of humankind as *imago Dei*, created in the image of God. What it means for men and women to be humans endowed with the divine image lies at the heart of this investigation.

Christian theology has historically located the *imago Dei* in various places, including rationality, relationality, responsibility, freedom, and historicity. In each of these cases, humankind as created, fallen, and redeemed has been the presuppositional foundation and defining linchpin according to which the doctrine has been constructed. Saying in what way humans are created by God and how that defines the human creature, what constitutes the fall of humanity, and how God's redemptive work in Jesus Christ manifests itself in a restored image of divinity in male and female is still the church's demanding task in this present day. The narrative method I propose and employ here enables a timely and responsible undertaking of that task.

Humankind as Created

What is it about our creation by God that makes us like God? What about us images God our Creator? While rationality, freedom, responsibility, relationality, and historicity are components of the human identity and experience which are in some important way reflective of God's own identity and experience, no one of those attributes expresses adequately the *imago Dei* and what Christian faith intends and needs to articulate and teach in relation to anthropology.

Much of classical Christian anthropology can still be affirmed by the church. Created by a good God, humankind, like all the rest of creation, is intrinsically good and thereby reflective of the good Creator. Created by God, creation is of God but not God. Without need to talk about substances and essences, Christian theology can affirm all that is not God as God's loved handiwork. As such, the creation is not independent but interdependent, contingent, and real. Ultimately related to God and penultimately related to all else including all others within and without the human species, humans are, with all else, God's valued creation. Symbiotically and intrinsically connected to the web of life of which all are part, the creation is worthy and valuable as God's intended world. Humans live and interact within this intricate, finely tuned, and sensitively balanced ecosystem. As conscious, free, intelligent, interactive, and responsible members of the creation, humans are endowed with both capacity for struggle and responsibility to struggle. This struggle, like God's with the primeval void and with concrete, historical evil, requires vision, imagination, courage, endurance, adventure, integrity, and interactivity. Like God's struggle, it is teleologically pointed toward wholeness understood as completion, justice, peace, joy, and Christ-like maturity. It is costly—for God, humans, and all the creation which also struggles toward divine harmony.

Humans are *imago Dei*: created with the capacity to struggle with problems of the human heart in conflict with itself, *humankind is capable of and responsible for creative, transforming struggle on behalf of all creation*. As creating partner with God the Creator, humankind strives alongside God to shape a world according to God's vision and intention of personal, social, and ecological wholeness and harmony. As the species conscious of itself and the rest of creation, humanity is accountable for divine-human creative work on behalf of other species with which we are joined in symbiotic interdependency. Enabled by God's Spirit to struggle with our internal conflicts of the heart and our external, concrete failures to engage the struggle faithfully, we can fulfill our divine calling of creative, transforming work *with God*. Consequently, humanity has the possibility of seeing God's face. Endowed with the possibility to struggle and prevail creatively, humans are those who can enjoy a quality of relationship metaphorically imaged as "seeing God's face." The struggle accepted, undertaken, and worthily waged meets God on an uncommon plane, deepening radically the relationship with God and making it a "face to face" interaction. Multiple biblical pictures repeatedly witness to this iconoclastic truth. We have already examined several of these; I would like now to turn to another.

Let us look at Moses, struggler in Egypt with his own sin of murder and later with the Pharaoh and his unwillingness to release the Hebrews in bondage, and struggler again in the wilderness sojourn with his people's pettiness and more serious idolatry and with his own impatience. Moses, paradigmatic liberator, the one who struggles with his conflicted heart and that of his fellows, is buried at last in Moab, and the Deuteronomic eulogy is tersely profound: "And there arose not a prophet since

114

in Israel like unto Moses, *whom the Lord knew face to face*" (Deut. 34:10, emphasis added).

In his volume entitled *Doctrine*, James McClendon comments on this face to face quality of relationship between God and Israel's liberator. McClendon remarks that there was more to the relationship than Moses' intimate knowledge of God; at stake was God's knowledge of Moses in such an intimate way. Something in Moses' life journey has opened a door for God's face to face knowledge of him, the man. "Such was the openness of the man that God could come to know Moses in this immediate way, 'as one man speaks to another' (Ex. 33:11)" (McClendon, 1994:317). McClendon reflects on this intimate interaction in the context of his discussion of the atonement, stressing atonement's costliness for God and humanity. He does not, however, connect costliness on humanity's side with the *imago Dei*. It is important, however, to make that connection, I believe, and to relate intimate relationship with God to the *imago Dei* and its nature as struggle. Like God who struggles with the darkness to bring forth light and thence a world, humankind struggles with its own conflicted heart and brings into being a lighted world on a finite, interdependent level.

Moses's life journey has been one of struggle against the dark angel all along the way. Like David after him, he is capable of great love and callous infidelity, of both expressing and dissipating his remarkable gifts. After each failure, he has renewed his course, becoming finally Israel's paradigmatic liberator, model for Jewish and Christian liberators even into this century. This Moses, *precisely for all these reasons*, is one whom God can know face to face. With such a one deep intimacy is possible *for God*. Moses never rejects the struggle, as did Cain who thereby removed himself from God's presence. Indeed, much to the contrary, Moses *so fully engages the struggle* that he thereby *enters* God's presence so intimately and immediately, "as one man speaks to another," as to warrant emphatic biblical reference to that fact in the Exodus and Deuteronomy passages cited. Like Jacob who succeeds him, Moses struggles mightily and prevails, concluding his long journey *wounded and blessed*, face to face companion to God.

Humanity as Fallen

Reference to Cain and his refusal to struggle with his guilty heart directs our reflection toward humankind's fallenness. Like the *imago Dei* itself, this second aspect of theological anthropolgy has been variously understood. Immaturity, ignorance, finitude, rebellion, and pride have been identified as the content of human fallenness. In some measure, all those attributes participate in the fall, it is true. But the Cain and Abel narrative shows most clearly the locus and content of fallenness for those created in the *imago Dei*. It is not immaturity, rebellion, or the other traits listed above which constitute the fall, but rather *arrogant refusal to struggle with darkness*, persevering until the blessing has been won and a godly name bestowed. *Therein lies humanity's fallenness.* Cain repeatedly spurns God's loving solicitude, God's offer of enablement to turn his unrepentant heart toward compassion and pity, remorse and restitution, for killing his brother Abel. Instead of engaging this dark struggle, Cain accuses God of unmercifulness and removes himself from the struggle, an act amounting effectually and literally to removing himself from the presence of God. Hence, there will be no face to face relationship for Cain with God. Refusing to struggle with his conflicted heart, Cain has *cast a shadow within himself* over the image of God's likeness; instead of battling the dark, he has shrouded himself in it and prefigured thereby his own impending death. Created *imago Dei*, in the image of God, Cain has forfeited the grandeur of his creaturehood.

Cain's story is humanity's story. His fallenness is ours. Refusing to struggle and to be "radically helped" by God, we participate in and perpetuate the fall. Letty Russell's short book, *Becoming Human*, describes the concept of radical help (Russell, 1982). Russell paints a picture of God as Helper and humans as helpers with God. God as divine Helper is One who radically helps humanity, through Christ, toward full humanness and wholeness. Refusal to be radically helped by God constitutes our sin. Cain refuses this radical help and descends into the state of fallenness.

Babette's Feast can again illumine our thought. The elderly, alienated Brothers and Sisters in Berlevaag for years have refused to struggle. Though faithful Christians on other fronts, they have languished in fallenness by refusing to be radically helped by

God's grace to struggle with their festering, conflicted hearts until the blessing is given. Hence, there has been no forgiveness of one another and no restoration as Brothers and Sisters truly. Their fellowship has ceased to be a community of care and mutual hospitality. Slander, deceit, and thievery, and the guilt attending those violations against the once-loved neighbor, have not been grappled with and overcome—until Babette's feast. Catalytically dislodging the old saints from their self-imposed estrangement, Babette's sacramental banquet becomes the divine-human help they need and slowly accept. Once engaged, their struggle toward reconciliation moves apace, however, and the night ends in joy and merriment, blessing and restored naming of friend, companion, cherished ones all, each to the other. Erstwhile brothers and sisters of Cain, they are now again those who they truly are, Brothers and Sisters in Christ, image of God, *imago Dei*.

Humanity as Redeemed

These restored ones of Dinesen's tale are examples of humanity as redeemed. They have accepted God's enabling grace for undertaking the struggle. Emerging limping but blessed, they resume their growth in compassion, love, mercy, hospitality, joy, and peace. Christians who had lost the joy of their salvation, they now revel in the divine miracle of a quality of companionship so intimate as to be expressed through the metaphor of face to face relationship. We might say that now they know and are known by God, as well as their neighbors, face to face.

This kind of intimacy is the meaning of humanity as redeemed, "at one" with God, neighbor, and self. Neighbors include the creation *beside* the human part of it, that is, standing *alongside* and symbiotically interconnected with the human species. Theology and church need now to investigate what a face to face relationship with the creation can mean, and already means in the heart and intention of God. How can we struggle to overcome our enmity with nature so that a quality of relating to the created order will be molded which God and we can claim as face to face? I believe that is our task in this present day of ecological peril. To be sure, we will emerge wounded and limping from this struggle. We can possibly emerge also blessed, and enabled to bless again the creation and all that is within it.

At one with God, humanity, ourselves, and all the creation of which we are part—this is the redemption of humanity and fullness of the *imago Dei*. Jesus is our exemplar, model, and power. Fully united to God and the world, Jesus lives all his life toward God's house and its hospitality, pouring out his gifts for that end. That which he most richly, truly is and thereby the best he has to offer is given lavishly for the divine-human glory of opening the doors of God's house and bidding those without to enter. Incarnating the meaning he preaches and teaches, Jesus models the hospitality of God's household in all he is and does. Storyteller extraordinaire, preacher, teacher, healer, face to face companion of God and all his fellows, Jesus embodies redemption and manifests God fully. Through living Jesus' story, the Christian also embodies redemption and images God, literally fleshing out the narrative journey of atonement and the reality of *imago Dei*.

The *imago Dei* is not rationality, relationality, historicity, freedom, or responsibility. These are components within a broader frame. The *imago Dei* is a dynamic, storied event showing what God is like through narrative journeying, which glorifies God in character, reconciliation, atonement, and the maturity of the fullness of Christ. Living this divine-human narrative, humans show themselves endowed with the divine image, an image of both wound and blessing, seen most revealingly in its cruciform starkness. What is the cross if not a wound? What is the cross if not a blessing? How the way there except through Gethsemane's dark night of struggle? Humankind as *imago Dei* is humankind as narrative journeyer, radically helped struggler, wounded and blessed face to face companion with God, prevailing against sin and injustice and opening God's house against the powers of darkness in all its forms.

PART III

Stories of Hope and Resurrection

Stories of hope and resurrection cannot be separated from stories of conflict and struggle. Resurrection has meaning only in relation to death. Hope has meaning only in relation to hopelessness. Hence, "problems of the human heart in conflict with itself" are the context for the church's stories of resurrection and hope. For that reason, in this third part of our study, we shall look again at certain of those stories we have examined, this time attending more closely to what they have to show us about the Christian hope and its grounding in the church's central mystery, the resurrection. And we shall look at other biblical stories which we have yet to examine.

First, however, because worship and discipleship are the crucial connecting link between biblical and other stories important to us in our theological exploration, in this section of our study, I wish to place our attention in a more focused manner on congregational story. Thus, before moving to the biblical narratives and again to *Babette's Feast*, I want to focus more directly on the church story at Watts Street Baptist Church, Mel Williams' preaching, and the narrative of worship and discipleship which the sisters and brothers of Watts Street live together. Let us look at another of Mel's sermons, this one entitled "The Messiah Is Among You." In this sermon, Mel recounts a story in William Bausch's *Storytelling: Imagination and Faith* and interlaces it with both the Emmaus Road story and the Watts Street Baptist congregational story. Mel's resurrection sermon of hope goes as follows:

> Let me tell you a story—one that is surely based on the Emmaus Road story. . . . There was once a famous monastery that had fallen on hard times.

In days past the monastery was filled with young monks. The church resounded with singing. There was a vibrance about the place. But now it was deserted. People no longer came there to be nourished by prayer. A handful of old monks shuffled through the cloisters and praised God with heavy hearts.

On the edge of the monastery woods, an old rabbi had built a little hut. He would come there from time to time to fast and pray. No one ever spoke with him; but whenever he appeared, the word would be passed from monk to monk: "The rabbi walks in the woods." And, for as long as he was there, the monks would feel sustained by his powerful presence.

One day the abbot of the monastery decided to visit the rabbi and open his heart to him. After the morning Eucharist, the abbot set out through the woods. As he approached the hut, the abbot saw the rabbi standing in the doorway, his arms outstretched to welcome him. It was as though he had been waiting for him. The two embraced like long-lost brothers.

After a while the rabbi asked the abbot to come inside and sit with him at the wooden table with the Scriptures open on it. They sat there for a moment in the presence of the Book. Then the rabbi began to cry. The abbot then covered his face and began to cry too. For the first time in his life, he cried his heart out.

After the tears had ceased to flow, and all was quiet, the rabbi lifted his head, "You and your brothers are serving God with heavy hearts," he said. "You have come here to ask a teaching of me. I will give you a teaching, but you can only repeat it once. After that, no one must ever say it aloud again."

The rabbi looked straight at the abbot and said, "The Messiah is among you." There was silence. Then the rabbi said, "Now you must go."

The abbot left without a word and without looking back.

The next morning the abbot called his monks together in the chapter room. He told them he had received a teaching from "the rabbi who walks in the woods," and this teaching was never again to be spoken aloud. Then he looked at each of the brothers and said, "The rabbi said that one of us is the Messiah."

The monks were startled. "What could it mean?" they all thought. "Is Brother John the Messiah? Is Father Matthew? Or Brother Thomas? Am I the Messiah? What could this mean?" They were all puzzled by the rabbi's teaching. But no one ever mentioned it again.

As time went by, the monks began to treat one another with a very special reverence. There was a gentle, wholehearted, human quality about them now which was hard to describe but easy to notice. They began now to study the Scriptures as people who were looking for something. Visitors to the monastery found themselves moved by the life of these monks. Before long, people were coming from far and wide to be nourished by the prayer life of the monks. And once again, young men were asking to become part of the community.

In those days, the rabbi no longer walked in the woods. His hut had fallen into ruins. But somehow or other, the old monks who heard his teaching felt sustained by his prayerful presence. (Williams, 1992; story from William Bausch, *Storytelling: Imagination and Faith*)

At this point, Mel continues his sermon by reflecting with the congregation on the story and interlacing it with theirs. Emphasizing that the story of the rabbi who walks in the woods is one of "conversion, change, [and] resurrection," Mel also points out that it is about hospitality. He then goes on to focus the congregation's attention on the connection of hospitality to their own experience of resurrection life.

Mel demonstrates that resurrection and hospitality are intimately joined. In the act of extending hospitality, the Emmaus Road travelers recognized the resurrected Messiah. In giving and receiving hospitality among themselves, the monks began to live a vibrant resurrection life, "and that hospitality began to have a ripple effect toward visitors and newcomers to their community." Drawing on the insights of Henri Nouwen, Mel adds that hospitality is a *spiritual* phenomenon having the peculiar quality of a kind of love that "creates a free and empty space." This "friendly emptiness" provides a safe and free space in which those who enter may find themselves and their own stories uncoerced by the host or by any others.

Mel Williams's ideas about hospitality and its relation to resurrection life need here to be joined to Douglas E. Wingeier's insights about the nature of Christ's reign. In an excellent publication entitled *Jesus Christ: Resurrection*, Wingeier tells the story of a modern-day family we all know in one way or another. What rivets our attention in this story is an uncommon quality of hospitality lived by the parents in relation to their adult daughters and sons. Nouwen's notion of "friendly emptiness" describes what these parents have been able to offer their children. Wingeier suggests that because of the quality of relationship

121

offered by these parents, Christ reigns in their story. Here is the narrative:

> This family has gone to church every Sunday. The parents raised their four children in the Sunday School, told them Bible stories, and taught them Christian moral standards. But they could not avoid the influences of the society in which they lived. The children in this family went to public schools, watched movies and television, and made friends among the children of other ordinary families. They live in a midwestern suburb, and three of their children have been educated in small liberal-arts colleges.
>
> Two of the children began smoking marijuana in high school and then got into harder drugs in college. One son took up selling drugs for a period but was frightened into giving that up when threatened with a knife by a man who refused to pay for his delivery. While in high school, the younger daughter was raped one night while walking home from work. All three older children had several casual sexual liaisons in college and later lived with someone of the opposite sex in longer-term relationships. One daughter had an abortion, and the other was several months pregnant when she got married. Despite their parents' urgings, only the youngest son remained active in church through high school. The two daughters never attend church. One is hostile to religion; and the other has taken up Eastern meditation, yoga, and theosophy. The older boy attends church when he is at home, but his faith encompasses elements of several religions and philosophies. Now in his midtwenties, he has not held a steady job for over three years.
>
> These parents are inclined to blame themselves for what has happened to their children, but they know that they are also victims of a massive cultural shift. The changes in our society have affected the best of families, leading them to ask whether anyone is in charge. Can we depend on anyone or anything in this sea of change? Whom can we trust? What is for sure? Are there any rules we can count on? Old rules, new rules—what has happened to God's rule?

· ·

So how does a contemporary Christian family that is tempted to ask whether anyone is in charge gain enough confidence that Christ reigns to be ready to "press on toward the goal"? The rules have been changed without our permission, and it is hard to see the rule of Christ through our confusion.

This may be no final solution, but here is what the parents

described earlier have tried to do. They have tried to stay in communication with their children, even though they disapproved of some of their behavior. The parents feel that loving their children is more important than condemning them. The parents have expressed appreciation for the choices and values they could approve. They have tried to accept their children's friends and welcome them into the family home.

The parents have shared their own religious beliefs and moral standards so their children have known when they violated their parents' convictions. But in doing so, they have taken care to respect the young people's beliefs and values and have left them free to make their own decisions. They have tried to stay open to learn from their children rather than insisting that they as parents [are] always right.

The result has been that, while family members still disagree, they also love and respect one another. They enjoy being together and discussing their contrasting views, even though the parents are still distressed at some of the children's behavior.

No two persons in this family of six acknowledge Christ's reign in the same way. But all share a commitment to the extension of love, peace, and justice in the world. They do not hold to the same standards of thought and behavior, but each in her or his own way accepts accountability to a Power beyond themselves. All believe in and strive for a better future, and all pour their energies into constructive ventures. (Wingeier, 1985:36,37,42,43)

All the foregoing stories are ingredient to the church story at Watts Street Baptist Church. They have functioned as part of the shaping worship and reflective experience of the body. Consequently, they have been formative for that church's ever-developing doctrines of Christ, church, and humankind. Mel's sermon with its interlaced Emmaus Road story, the story of the rabbi and monks, and Henri Nouwen's notion of "friendly emptiness," along with Douglas Wingeier's story of the family struggling to remain in respectful communication with one another have all been vital resources for Watts Street Baptist's theological reflection. The nature of the risen Christ's reign has been illuminated for the faithful there by these interlacing stories.

As a theologian, as well as a former member of Watts Street Baptist, my work in setting forth the church's doctrine, writing about it and teaching it, has been substantially shaped by these shared experiences with others of that faith community. Thus so, I have been a theologian standing within the circle of faith. With my pastor's help, I have been enabled in understanding the centrality of hospitality. A gifted theologian himself, Mel Williams has been an important theological conversation partner for me.

What, then, is the yield from these stories for our project here? Let us recapitulate briefly some things we have already discussed. Christology and anthropology in a narrative perspective take the form of storytelling by showing that Jesus' own life was a story unfolded in light of what it means to live within God's house and to enable the entrance of others into that house as well. The journey to God's house is fraught with struggle; each journeyer must contend with the dark angel and problems of the human heart in its conflict. The prevailing struggler, though permanently marked or wounded, is rewarded with seeing God face to face and the gift of a new name. To see God's face and to bear a new name are to have entered a life style and attitudinal realm of compassion, love, courage, pity, endurance, justice, and peace. We need to add one thing more—hospitality.

Life in God's house has to do with hospitality. The redeemed life of the Christian opens up space for others to be, a space where they can develop their best gifts and give those back to God and the world in genuine self-sacrifice. The "friendly emptiness" of that space offers both protection and freedom. The weary and frightened can rest there and be enfolded there. They can dine on food and wine in jubilation. They can dare to hold different views and embrace different standards and values, and they can communicate those to other guests in the house without fear of condemnation. The family Wingeier described has learned about hospitality. The parents do not assume that they alone are to teach but know that they also need to be taught. Their willingness to listen to their sons and daughters and to respect their different views does not mean that they have forfeited their own values in an effort of appeasement. Instead, in the family home, they are hospitable hosts who have opened space for their offspring's full adulthood and are enjoying the enriched relationship and communication thus made possible. In a real sense, they are being Jesus to their children. They are treating them as Jesus would treat them. *And* they are receiving Christ through their sons and daughters. They have clearly stated their own perspectives and

124

values and are working not to feel guilty because their sons and daughters have rejected much that they taught them. Perhaps most importantly, they have not assumed that their values are the only valid ones. Change for parents and sons and daughters is facilitated in this hospitable environment. But no one's agenda is to change the other into his or her likeness. The "friendly emptiness" of their home strikes us with its compelling attractiveness. We sense that it is like unto the house of God. We sense that this is Christ's reign.

Let us return to Mel Williams' sermon. Continuing to reflect on Nouwen's theology of hospitality, Mel states:

> In the same way, teachers should show hospitality to students, giving them space to do their own growing, to ask and answer their own questions. Physicians and counselors should show hospitality to their clients, listening, making space for them to tell their own stories and find their own healing.
>
> Against this background, the story of Emmaus Road and [the story of] the Rabbi Who Walks in the Woods have led me back to the story of the Last Judgment in Matthew 25.
>
> You may remember that here Jesus says people will be divided into two groups—those on the right hand and those on the left. The difference is that those on the right hand had been hospitable.
>
> When did we see you hungry and thirsty? When did we see you a stranger and welcome you? Or naked . . . or sick . . . or in prison? Those on the right hand were the ones who showed hospitality to the hungry, the thirsty, the stranger, the naked, the sick, the prisoner. They had not tried to change them. They had simply fed them, given them drink, offered them welcome and dignity, clothed them, visited them—offered them a free and friendly space in which to seek their own solutions.
>
> Those of the left hand were surely concerned too. But they likely had felt that the hungry, the thirsty, the stranger, the sick, the prisoner were probably undeserving. If and when they would straighten up and fly right and conform to our values, then of course we would reward them with our help.
>
> The point of the story (and our earlier stories) is that Jesus comes to us in disguise. 'Inasmuch as you did it to the least of these, you did it to me.'
>
> . . . .
>
> Now and again the risen Lord walks with us in the midst of ordinary activities: walking down the street, sitting in church,

talking with a stranger. He is in disguise. If we can learn again to practice the ancient custom of hospitality, we may entertain him unawares. (Williams, 1992:4)

Stories of hope, renewal, and resurrection show themselves to be stories of hospitality, as the Emmaus Road story demonstrates. It will be worthwhile for us to examine more closely the connection between resurrection and hospitality. We have already seen that hospitality is what happens in God's house. As a place of hospitality, God's house is a haven where weary people rest and hungry people eat with fulfillment and joy. It is a house where they delight in the companionship of the host and one another. And significantly, as Nouwen suggests, it is a place of "friendly emptiness" where mutually respectful companions find space to be who they are. At least part of the meaning of resurrection, and an important part, is resurrection to hospitality in God's world house. Worship at Watts Street Baptist has provided a connecting link enabling us to achieve clarity about this vital truth. Interlacing several narratives in his sermon on the resurrection, Mel Williams created a context of worship and reflection which illuminated the nature of both resurrection and hospitality and the intrinsic relation between the two.

Hebrew-Christian scriptures are replete with stories of hospitality, though the word itself is never used. Contained in the New Testament are numerous stories of Jesus' blessing and rewarding others' acts of hospitality, condemning the failure of hospitality, and clearly calling his hearers to life characterized by hospitality. The Hebrew Bible contains many like narratives wherein God's spokespersons sound the same message and call.

Among those stories of Jesus' blessing and rewarding of hospitality are the parables of the Last Judgment, the Good Samaritan, the story of Mary and Martha, and the story of the Woman at the Well. Among the stories in which Jesus indicts those who fail to extend hospitality to him and others are the story of Jesus' reproach of Simon for withholding from him customary hospitality for the guest, again the Parable of the Last Judgment, and again the Parable of the Good Samaritan, the Parable of the Rich Man and Lazarus, and the story of the woman taken in adultery.

In the Sermon on the Mount, Jesus calls his listeners to a life lived according to God's hospitality; the Beatitudes set forth the way of such a life. Jesus' exhortations to love and pray for the enemy, as well as the brother who is seen and still unforgiven and unloved, are calls to resurrection hospitality.

Whenever we think of hospitality, we usually think also of food, do we not? The connection between hospitality and food is intrinsic. The *com-panion* to whom we offer hospitality and from whom we gratefully receive hospitality is the one with whom we eat bread. The etymology itself of the word companion conveys this reality. If we transpose these thoughts to the nexus of hospitality, food, *and resurrection*, where does this line of thinking lead us? Again, *worship and discipleship are the generative connecting link for our reflection.* Here, we find ourselves at the heart of the church and its faith expressed in liturgical, performative act—*the Lord's Supper.* In worshiping at the Lord's Table, we express gratitude for the self-sacrifice of Jesus and celebrate his resurrection by partaking of the bread and wine and serving it to our companions. What shall we do with this rich and marvelous reality? Christian theology has not at all exhausted the deep and profound richness of what occurs at the Lord's Table. I propose that we continue the methodology we have applied up to this point and interlace biblical narratives, particularly that of the Last Supper, with *Babette's Feast* and other narratives to find where hope, renewal, and resurrection most richly transform our personal and corporate stories, making us resurrection people in our day. Before proceeding along that course, however, we need to consider another important body of work informative for what we are attempting here.

At this point, I wish to introduce recent work of James Wm. McClendon's which is pertinent to our task. At the time I began writing this book, McClendon was engaged in writing the second volume of his three-volume systematic theology. The first, *Ethics*, was published in 1986 by Abingdon Press. The second, *Doctrine*, also published by Abingdon in 1994, is one which I have been privileged to read in manuscript form. McClendon sets forth in this baptist theology a method informed by the work of Alasdair McIntyre and the early twentieth-century philosopher Wittgenstein. Here, McClendon fashions a model of Christian practice—particularly the practice of doctrine—which has also been influenced by the thought of George Lindbeck and others whom he acknowledges. According to McClendon's model, the Lord's

Supper is a practice of the church constituted by four important elements: end, participants, means, and rules. By examining with McClendon the Christian practice of the Eucharist, or as baptists prefer, the Lord's Supper, we can understand better the congregational, liturgical link between biblical narratives and our many other narratives and the *constitutive, indispensable role congregational practices play in the origination of valid and authentic doctrine.*

In *Ethics* McClendon asserts unequivocally that only doctrine engendered by the church's "original practices," meaning not the church's first practices, but church practices which originate or give birth to, doctrine, is valid (McClendon, 1986:181). Doctrine spun out of the abstract environs of the academy fails to remain connected to the church's lived story, its formative practices and virtues, and thereby loses vitality and validity. Doctrine which, on the other hand, grows out of the faith community's true worship and discipleship—namely, its faithful *practices* of preaching, teaching, Lord's Supper, and baptism—is faithful doctrine, valid and vital.

In endorsing the perspective set forth by McClendon, I am offering, as well, a view which has commonality with Ronald Thiemann's. Like McClendon's and Thiemann's, my work attempts to be descriptive, normative, non-foundational theology which pays "close attention to the patterns inherent in particular beliefs and practices rather than to a general theory which norms all religious discourse." (Thiemann, 1985/1987:72)

How, then, does McClendon set forth the practices model? Attention needs first to be given to the four elements of practices: *end, participants, means, and rules.* Christian, congregational practices which originate doctrine finally point toward one *end* or goal: the maturity of the community of faith measured according to the full stature of Jesus Christ. " . . . until all of us come to the unity of the faith and of the knowledge of the Son of God, to maturity, to the measure of the full stature of Christ" (Ephesians 4:13). All the practices the church enacts in its lived expression including baptism, Lord's Supper, proclamation, witness, ministry to the poor and a ravaged creation, and other practices have as their goal this unity, knowledge, and maturity. This maturity, we might heed, is nothing less than the maturity of Christ, that "full stature." This is the *end* or goal of all that the church is and does.

Who are the *participants* in these practices? Only those who

128

intend to participate qualify; mere spectators or those mildly interested cannot be considered participants. Attitude and intention to participate are essential for candidates, and are exemplified in steps which the aspiring participant takes. Most significantly these include catechetical preparation and baptism, themselves formative practices which begin the Christian journey.

The *means* employed in practices are determined by the nature of the practice itself. Since we are considering the practice of the Lord's Supper particularly, it is helpful to consider the means employed for the practice of this sacrament. Means include the serving and taking of bread and wine or unfermented grape juice, and the offering of prayers of blessing, institution, and thanksgiving.

The *rules* for the practice of the Lord's Supper include, negatively, prohibitions against gluttony, greed, and insincerity, and, positively, the participation of those who have entered the Christian community of faith through baptism.

In the following pages, we shall focus on the church's formative practice of Lord's Supper and its transformative correlative, discipleship and ministry. Now we need to pick up the theme, already introduced, which lies at the heart of discipleship and ministry—hospitality. Christology—and thereby anthropology—are, at core, hospitality. Jesus invites us into God's house, opening the doors of hospitality to God's world house *and* otherworld house of salvation, transformation, rest, jubilation, and life. Faithful discipleship and ministry do the same thing, joining Christ in this hospitable act in faithfulness to God and thanksgiving for God's own gracious acts.

Our study of the practice of the Lord's Supper will now be conducted through interlacing various biblical narratives beginning with the Last Supper narrative, the church's liturgical practice of the Lord's Supper, its discipleship and ministry corresponding to that formative practice, and literary and other artistic representations of the Lord's Supper. Our effort will be to understand more clearly Christ's identity and work—and thereby our own—as well as the nature of faithful discipleship and ministry, and finally, valid doctrine which critiques, corrects, and expresses the lived, congregational practice. At the end of this process, we should have a clearer understanding of the link between "original practices" and doctrine.

Interlacing will be done by superimposing picture upon picture to gain depth, detail, richness, and variety. Along with the practices model, McClendon offers a pictures model. In discussing eschatology, he recommends that the reader of scripture attend to the many and varied pictures of the end time which the Bible contains. Indeed, McClendon objects, it is unacceptable for us to pick one or two favorite pictures; rather, faithfulness requires us to bring all the pictures together and to negotiate an interpretation according to the centrality of Christ and the resurrection. McClendon believes the many pictures of the end time described in the Bible need to be understood in light of the "master" picture of the Lamb slain and risen. (McClendon, 1994:101)

Following McClendon's recommendation, I shall superimpose biblical pictures of hospitality one on the other, enabling the discovery of detail, nuance, color, depth, and richness and leading back to the picture with which we began, the Last Supper in the upper room. Along the way, we shall see the final gospel scene of hospitality in the upper room foreshadowed and partially expressed in other biblical pictures of hospitality which form its context. Interlaced with the biblical pictorial narratives, the church's worship experience of the Lord's Supper and the contemporary narrative *Babette's Feast* will further enrich the interpretative matrix out of which we examine, critique, and form anew our doctrinal affirmation of discipleship and ministry. Here, then, we shall find ourselves located in stories of hope, renewal, and resurrection.

Superimposing the somewhat different pictures in the synoptics upon one another, and the picture in John upon those, we get a richly nuanced composite of the biblical pictures of the Last Supper. Jesus carefully prepares the Passover meal and, like a sensitive and good host, invites his guests to join him in the preparations. His disciples are made to feel that they are contributing to an important shared event. At some point during the meal the disciples begin to bicker over which of them is greatest. Jesus remonstrates that greatness is measured in terms of service and he himself is their servant. Perhaps it is at this point (the timing is unclear) that Jesus arises from the table, removes his outer robe, ties a towel around his waist, and proceeds to wash the feet of his friends. Performing the hospitality rite of the host for his invited and respected guests, Jesus cleans and soothes their travel-weary feet. Sharing bread and wine, food and companionship, Jesus creates a place of hospitality where the needs of all can be expressed, examined and talked about, and cared for.

The "friendly emptiness" where each can struggle toward his or her own solutions is created even for Judas whom Jesus challenges but does not block and who is permitted space to make even his tragic decisions. Jesus creates in a context of hospitality a final time of close communion for himself and the small band of followers who have traveled and ministered with him. Later, in Gethsemane and at Golgotha, they will be with him, more or less, but at this Passover meal, Jesus and they pass the cup and bread among themselves, laugh and talk, serve and are served. The disciples and Jesus struggle with who they and he are and what each must decide within his own heart to do. In this freighted but liberated context, Jesus institutes what we now know as the Lord's Supper. Significantly, hospitality and faithful discipleship and ministry are conjoined and prefigured for future days and future disciples.

In the midst of the supper, the issue of service and how it is rendered flows naturally out of the hospitable context itself. Already, before the church is constituted, the formative practice of Lord's Supper and its correlative transformative practice of discipleship and ministry are taking shape.

> Then he took a loaf of bread, and when he had given thanks, he broke it and gave it to them, saying, "This is my body, which is given for you. Do this in remembrance of me." And he did the same with the cup after supper, saying, "This cup that is poured out for you is the new covenant in my blood. . . .the greatest among you must become like the youngest, and the leader like one who serves. . . . I am among you as one who serves." (Luke 22:19, 20, 26b, 27b)

Girded with a towel and with basin in hand, Jesus role plays what it means for his disciples to remember him. He shows how breaking and eating the bread and drinking from the cup play out in the context of discipleship and ministry where service is enacted.

Where else does Jesus employ the means of hospitality—food and drink—to teach the meaning of life in God's house? Other pictures of hospitality come readily to mind. Moving back from this picture near the end of Jesus' journey to earlier pictures along the way, we see him feeding the five thousand, inviting guests to God's banquet table through parabolic story, celebrating the return of the prodigal son to his father's house and the feast awaiting him, receiving the hospitality of Mary and Martha in their home, extolling the hospitality of the Good Samaritan, both enjoying and contributing to the jubilant hospitality of the marriage celebration at Cana, and telling the gripping story of the Last Judgment in terms of hospitality given and withheld.

Finally, superimposed on all these pictures is the picture of Jesus himself as very Bread and Water of life. "Jesus said to them, 'I am the bread of life. Whoever comes to me will never be hungry, and whoever believes in me will never be thirsty'"(John 6:35). "Jesus said to her, 'Everyone who drinks of this water will be thirsty again, but those who drink of the water that I will give them will never be thirsty. The water that I will give will become in them a spring of water gushing up to eternal life'" (John 4:13,14). Jesus is himself God's hospitality, the meaning and content of life in God's house. This had been adumbrated at the very beginning of Jesus' public ministry in his baptism. John the Baptist, preparing the way for Jesus, had quoted Isaiah:

> Every valley shall be filled, and every mountain and hill shall be made low, and the crooked shall be made straight, and the rough ways made smooth, and all flesh shall see the salvation of God. (Luke 3:5–6)

In confirmation of this eschatological promise yet to be fulfilled, Luke simply states:

> Now when all the people were baptized, and when Jesus also had been baptized and was praying, the heaven was opened, and the Holy Spirit descended upon him in bodily form like a dove. And a voice came from heaven, "You are my Son, the Beloved; with you I am well pleased." (Luke 3:21–22)

Within this kaleidoscopic overview of many scriptural pictures, let us look more closely at certain pictures of hospitality and banqueting before converging again at the picture of the Last Supper. On numerous occasions, as we have seen, Jesus calls his followers to a table of banqueting, or he focuses their attention on scenes of banqueting and hospitality. From those early days in the Jerusalem temple while Mary and Joseph searched anxiously for him, Jesus has been guided by a vision of his father's house, the house of God. Consequently, his ministry has consistently fleshed out that vision. The stories he tells, the admonitions he voices, and the promises he extends, all express that vision. "Come unto me all ye that labor and are heavy laden and I will give you rest. . . . In my Father's house are many rooms. . . . When I was hungry, you gave me food, when I was a stranger, you welcomed me. . . ."

Let us examine the parable of the prodigal son. In *Speaking in Parables* Sallie McFague helps us become aware of the multiple juxtaposed images of starving and feasting through which Jesus tells this story (McFague, 1975). The younger brother squanders his inheritance in a far country and nearly dies of starvation, but when he goes home to his father's house, he enters a time and place of feasting. I have intentionally not said that when he returns to his father's house, he *returns again* to a time and a place of feasting. Nothing in the story permits us to conclude that such a feast had been given there before. I realize the danger of stretching this idea too far, but perhaps we might say that all had not been well in this house in the past. There are suggestions of strained relations among the members of the family. We might even imagine that when the son returns, relationships are renegotiated, not as he had rehearsed in his nervous role-playing on the way home, but in a way which recognizes that he is a different person now and all the members of the household are different, as well. With respect for one another and their differences (we have hope for the older brother) giving content to their love, these people are ready for hospitable, life-giving relationships. They are ready to kill the fatted calf and make merry.

In the Prodigal Son parable, extravagant hospitality characterizes the father's response to his son's homecoming, and a like extravagance marks the hospitality of the good Samaritan. Having rescued the injured man from certain death, the good Samaritan takes him to an inn, pays for lodging, food, and medical care, and opens a charge account in his behalf. By teaching his followers through these narratives, Jesus foreshadows his own extravagant upper room washing of his disciples' feet and, finally, his crucifixion and resurrection themselves. Set in the context of hospitality, these word pictures provide an image of the nature and meaning of discipleship and ministry.

Superimposing picture upon picture (this has been the scripture writers' method before it was ours) and holding together images of dining and God's house, we see another example in the Lukan narrative setting forth the parable of the Great Dinner against the backdrop of Jesus' attendance at a sabbath meal in the "house of a leader of the Pharisees." Jesus immediately notices the scrambling for seats of honor and addresses the situation, admonishing the anxious guests to practice humility in where they choose to seat themselves. Their concern should not be self-exaltation but willingness to take a seat at the table not designated for the guest of honor. Having spoken thus to the guests, who evidently are the able and privileged friends and associates of the host, Jesus then addresses the host himself, enjoining him to open his doors to those who are poor and lame and to spread his table for those who are crippled and blind. Jesus is addressing the issue of hospitality and its relation to life in God's house.

At this point, Jesus makes direct reference to the resurrection. Food, drink, hospitality, and service to the poor and disadvantaged are dynamically connected, Jesus implies, to participation in the resurrection of the righteous. "But when you give a banquet, invite the poor, the crippled, the lame, and the blind. And you will be blessed, because they cannot repay you, for you will be repaid at the resurrection of the righteous" (Luke 14:13–14).

An excited dinner guest responds to Jesus, "Blessed is anyone who will eat bread in the kingdom of God!" It is at this time that Jesus, continuing the theme of resurrection, relates the parable of the Great Dinner. All those invited who are wealthy enough to purchase land and yokes of oxen, and those who have the resources to undertake marriage, reject the invitation. Again, Jesus focuses his hearers' attention on the issue of discipleship and service to the lowly. "Go out at once into the streets and lanes of the town and bring in the poor, the crippled, the blind, and the lame" (Luke 14:21b). Jesus suggests that, even then, there will be ample room in God's house for all who will come in. And, Jesus intimates parabolically, God wishes the house to be filled completely.

The writer of the Lucan narrative has superimposed picture upon picture of dinners, dining, and refusals to dine, beginning with Jesus' attendance at a sabbath dinner in a Pharisee's house.

Doing so, he has foreshadowed the Passover meal to come and partly expressed the struggle among the disciples over who would be greatest. Most importantly, the evangelist has connected hospitality and discipleship and shown these to be integrally connected to the resurrection. Therein, the Lucan narratives, we see, are narratives of hope, hospitality, renewal, and resurrected life.

Before returning to the Last Supper narrative and other New Testament narratives, we need to examine the Hebrew scriptures for similar narratives of hospitality. We could turn to a number of such pictures, but let us look at two, the stories of Joseph and Ruth. Like the story of the prodigal son, the story of Joseph and his brothers is replete with images of famine and feasting, dying and living. Famine has reached the land of Canaan and Jacob sends ten of his sons to Egypt to buy grain, "that we may live and not die" (Genesis 42:2b). At first, Joseph withholds the life-giving hospitality which can save his brothers and father from death. He pretends to believe his brothers are spies. In what appears to our modern eyes to be manipulative game-playing, Joseph tortures them with demands that they leave a hostage with him and bring Benjamin as proof of their honesty. Though he gives his brothers grain and even returns their money surreptitiously, Joseph's actions at this point are scarcely hospitable ones. While it is unclear whether he intends to teach them a lesson, hopes to evoke repentance for their injury to him so many years ago, or simply wishes to get Benjamin to Egypt, Joseph's actions toward his brothers are not commendable until Judah tells the story of Jacob's great suffering over the loss of his son (Joseph) and fear of losing Benjamin in like manner. At this point, however, Joseph's heart is thoroughly broken and, without waiting for words of repentance and entreaties of forgiveness, Joseph falls on his brothers' necks and weeps "so loudly that the Egyptians heard it, and the household of pharaoh heard it" (Genesis 45:2). Like the father in the parable of the Prodigal Son, Joseph responds with extravagant feeling and gracious hospitality. He confronts them directly, "I am your brother, Joseph, whom you sold into Egypt" (Genesis 45:4b). And he extends forgiveness even before it is sought. "And now do not be distressed, or angry with yourselves, because you sold me here; for God sent me before you to preserve life" (Genesis 45:5).

Famine and plenty are juxtaposed in the Joseph narrative, and hospitality is the midwife of transformation and reconciliation. A family's story of partiality, jealousy, arrogance, hate, injury, secrecy, guilt, and estrangement is reclaimed and restored through love made concrete and given content in hospitality. The "dead" Joseph is resurrected for the grieving Jacob, and a dying family narrative is resurrected to new vigor and wholeness.

> For the famine has been in the land these two years; and there are five more years in which there will be neither plowing nor harvest. God sent me before you to preserve for you a remnant on earth, and to keep alive for you many survivors. So it was not you who sent me here, but God; . . . . Hurry and go up to my father and say to him . . . "come down to me, do not delay. You shall settle in the land of Goshen, and you shall be near me, you and your children and your children's children, as well as your flocks, your herds, and all that you have. I will provide for you there—since there are five more years of famine to come—so that you and your household, and all that you have, will not come to poverty."
>
> "And now your eyes and the eyes of my brother Benjamin see that it is my own mouth that speaks to you. You must tell my father how greatly I am honored in Egypt, and all that you have seen. Hurry and bring my father down here." Then he fell upon his brother Benjamin's neck and wept, while Benjamin wept upon his neck. And he kissed all his brothers and wept upon them; and after that his brothers talked with him. (Genesis 45:6–15)

When we superimpose the picture of hospitality in the story of Ruth upon this one in the story of Joseph and interlace these Old Testament pictures with the biblical pictures we have already seen in the New Testament, depth is enlarged, detail is highlighted, and multiple nuances are teased out and expanded. Again, the drama of famine and plenty, starving and feasting, and the restorative power of hospitality fill the stage. In the story of Ruth, Naomi, and Boaz, hospitality is the originative context for new forms of hospitality yet to emerge. The nature of the relation between Naomi and Ruth is one of hospitality in its profoundest expression. Left destitute by the death of their husbands, both women must find a way to survive, but mere survival is never their central concern. Each regards the welfare of the other as well as her own well-being. Naomi extends to Ruth and Orpah, her second daughter-in-law, the "friendly emptiness" of genuine hospitality which allows them to find their own solution to their problems. Intending at first to take her daughters-in-law back to Judah with her, Naomi instead frees them to find their own course, and possibly to find new husbands in Moab:

> But Naomi said to her daughters-in-law, "Go back each of you to your mother's house. May the Lord deal kindly with you, as you have dealt with the dead and with me. The Lord grant that you may find security, each of you in the house of your husband." Then she kissed them and they wept aloud. They said to her, "No, we will return with you to your people." But Naomi said, "Turn back, my daughters, why will you go with me? Do I still have sons in my womb that they may become your husbands? Turn back, my daughters, go your way, for I am too old to have a husband. . . . Then they wept aloud again. Orpah kissed her mother-in-law, but Ruth clung to her. (Ruth 1:8–14)

Ruth's own response to Naomi is one of hospitality, the intention to share lodging, companions, and destiny with the woman who is both friend and mother-in-law to her.

> Do not press me to leave you
>   or to turn back from following you!
> Where you go, I will go;
>   Where you lodge, I will lodge;
> your people shall be my people,
>   and your God my God.
>   Where you die, I will die—
>   there will I be buried.
> May the Lord do thus and so to me,
>   and more as well,
> if even death parts me from you! (Ruth 1:16–17)

Reconciled to sharing their lot fully, Naomi and Ruth journey on to the land of Judah. There, Ruth is able to secure food for herself and Naomi by gleaning behind the reapers. She gleans in a field belonging to Boaz, a kinsman of her deceased father-in-law, Elimelech. Boaz treats her with uncommon hospitality:

> Then Boaz said to Ruth, "Now listen, my daughter, do not go to glean in another field or leave this one, but keep close to my young women. Keep your eyes on the field that is being reaped, and follow behind them. I have ordered the young men not to bother you. If

you get thirsty, go to the vessels and drink from what the young men have drawn. (Ruth 2:8–9)

Overwhelmed by Boaz's gracious reception of her, Ruth inquires how it is that she has attracted such favorable treatment. Boaz's response acknowledges Ruth's hospitality to her mother-in-law and implies that the hospitality extended by her to Naomi has reaped hospitality for herself.

All that you have done for your mother-in-law since the death of your husband has been fully told me, and how you left your father and mother and your native land and came to a people that you did not know before. May the Lord reward you for your deeds, and may you have a full reward from the Lord, the God of Israel, under whose wings you have come for refuge!

. . . .

When she got up to glean, Boaz instructed his young men, "Let her glean even among the standing sheaves, and do not reproach her. You must also pull out some handfuls for her from the bundles, and leave them for her to glean, and do not rebuke her. (Ruth 2:11–12; 15–16)

The story of Ruth's and Naomi's hospitality to each other, and Boaz's hospitality to Ruth ends with a paean of praise to God whose divine hospitality is source of theirs.

So Boaz took Ruth and she became his wife. When they came together, the Lord made her conceive, and she bore a son. Then the women said to Naomi, "Blessed be the Lord, who has not left you this day without next-of-kin; and may his name be renowned in Israel! He shall be to you a restorer of life and a nourisher of your old age; for your daughter-in-law who loves you, who is more to you than seven sons, has borne him." Then Naomi took the child and laid him in her bosom, and became his nurse. The women of the neighborhood gave him a name, saying, "A son has been born to Naomi." They named him Obed; he became the father of Jesse, the father of David (Ruth 4:13–17).

Naomi, like Jacob, has had her life restored to her in her old age. Resurrection has happened, and famine has given way to plenty, death to new birth, and hopelessness to hope. Again, the pattern is recognized; from death to resurrection to the table of the Lord and its plenty in the house of God.

With these pictures from the Hebrew Bible, and there are

numerous others, let us return to the early Christian scriptures and the most signal narrative of hospitality divine and human in all Christian writing, the parable of the Final Judgment in the Matthean gospel. We have already seen how Mel Williams in his Easter sermon connected this premier story with the central themes of hospitality and resurrection. This narrative of God's final evaluation of the human story bears another look. How has its meaning eluded us? Now that we have interlaced numerous stories, it seems clear, obvious even, that Jesus' parable is about hospitality given and withheld. Perhaps it has simply been too much for us to absorb, this notion that entrance into God's house and life everlastingly lived there hangs on whether we, with God, have shaped our discipleship and ministry along the lines of hospitality. Yet the simplicity of the parable confounds us with its stark elegance and depth, its unadorned profundity. Entering and living in God's world house, and otherworld house, has to do with inviting other strangers in. It has to do with simple but essential things like drink, food, shelter, clothing, comfort, and acceptance—hospitality. Jesus is clear:

> When the Son of Man comes in his glory, and all the angels with him, then he will sit on the throne of his glory. All the nations will be gathered before him, and he will separate people one from another as a shepherd separates the sheep from the goats, and he will put the sheep at his right hand and the goats at the left. Then the king will say to those at his right hand, 'Come, you that are blessed by my Father, inherit the kingdom prepared for you from the foundation of the world; for I was hungry and you gave me food, I was thirsty and you gave me something to drink, I was a stranger and you welcomed me, I was naked and you gave me clothing, I was sick and you took care of me, I was in prison and you visited me.' Then the righteous will answer him, 'Lord, when was it that we saw you hungry and gave you food, or thirsty and gave you something to drink? And when was it that we saw you a stranger and welcomed you, or naked and gave you clothing? And when was it that we saw you sick or in prison and visited you?' And the king will answer them, 'Truly I tell you, just as you did it to one of the least of these who are members of my family, you did it to me.'(Matthew 25:31–40)

Those on the right hand are astonished to learn that they are welcomed into God's eternal house on the basis of their own

139

welcoming acts! They learn, as well, that God thinks in explicitly familial terms and identifies as family member with family member in relation to the lowly and outcast, those most in need of hospitality. They are the very members of God's own family: "Truly I tell you, just as you did it to one of the least of these who are members of my family, you did it to me" (Matthew 25:40).

Jim McClendon has elucidated the uncalculated nature of the hospitable deeds of these members of God's family. (McClendon, 1986:59). This uncalculated response to human need calls to mind for me a story which I have named my "mustard biscuits" story. I have alluded to this story in part I; now, I wish to tell it in its entirety. The protagonist of the story is my mother, Annie Mote Barnes.

> Devola Butler was brown-haired, green-eyed, and freckle-faced, and I wasn't sure I liked her. Devola had seven brothers and sisters besides her mother and father, Mae and Charlie Butler. And the ten of them lived in a two-bedroom cotton mill house about a block from us in Bladenboro, North Carolina. The Butler children were hungry. Charlie was the only one in the family who worked and Mae stayed home with the children. Unlike our family with two incomes and only three in the house, the Butlers had to stretch Charlie's cotton mill wages to feed and clothe Eunice, Eugene, Devola, and all the rest. That meant the food generally ran out before Charlie's paycheck came in. So, my mother often heard a small knock at our screen door and the plea, "Miss Annie, can I have a mustard biscuit?" Whether it was Devola or Eugene or one of the other Butler kids, Mama always answered that question by turning back to the stove, reaching into the oven, drawing out a biscuit homemade at breakfast, slicing it in two, spreading it with French's prepared mustard, and placing it in the outstretched hand. I never knew her to turn a hungry Butler child away from our screen door.
>
> On Sundays, Mama took me with her to New Light Free Will Baptist Church (we attended a Free Will Baptist Church until I was seven) at the end of our dirt street. There, I heard her sing and pray with the other grownups, and sometimes I saw her shout. All of it had to do

with Jesus. I learned early that Mama loved Jesus and depended on him for all kinds of things from the healing of a bad infection from a caesarian section when my baby brother was born dead, to protection from a heavy electrical storm, to more flour and mustard for the mustard biscuits. Mama loved Jesus, and she loved to sing his story as she scrubbed our clothes on her aluminum washboards. Mama loved Jesus, and she loved to hear the Reverend Mr. Kelly Coleman and the Reverend Mrs. Zellie Thompson preach the story at New Light Free Will Baptist. And gradually, I came to realize that all the preaching and praying and singing and shouting had something to do with mustard biscuits and the Butler children.

"Mustard Biscuits" has become for me a paradigmatic story for showing what it means to live the story of Jesus, and I often tell it to my theology classes. I suspect that they do not long remember much about ontological dualisms and metaphysical systems, but I have a notion that my students remember the story of "Mustard Biscuits."

McClendon's point that the merciful acts recorded in Matthew 25 were unreckoned acts of caring, uncalculated, flowing from the redeemed heart of the just has relevance here (McClendon, 1986:59). I doubt very much that my mother ever gave a thought to her mustard biscuits and their place in the kingdom of God. Certainly, she never imagined that they were *given to* God. All she knew was that she was giving a hungry Butler child a biscuit.

The pattern again manifests itself unmistakably: from death to resurrection to the table of the Lord and its plenty in the house of God. Death to stinginess and hardness of heart, and resurrection to life, food for the hungry, full and abundant life in *God's* house. But those who have withheld hospitality from the hungry, rejected, and sick have closed the doors of God's house even against themselves. Unwilling to welcome others, they have banished themselves.

Finally, let us superimpose one more picture of hospitality and feasting on the biblical pictures we have already examined, the picture of the eschatological feast, the marriage supper of the Lamb slain and risen.

Then I heard what seemed to be the voice of a great multitude, like the sound of many waters and like the sound of mighty thunderpeals, crying out,
"Hallelujah!
For the Lord our God
    the Almighty reigns,
Let us rejoice and exult
    and give him the glory,
for the marriage of the Lamb has come,
    and his bride has made herself ready;
to her it has been granted to be clothed
with fine linen, bright and pure"—
for the fine linen is the righteous deeds of the saints.
    And the angel said to me, "Write this: Blessed are those who are invited to the marriage supper of the Lamb." And he said to me, "These are true words of God." Then I fell down at his feet to worship him, but he said to me, "You must not do that! I am a fellow servant with you and your comrades who hold the testimony of Jesus. Worship God! For the testimony of Jesus is the spirit of prophecy." (Revelation 19:6–10)

The marriage supper of the Lamb is held in a new heaven and a new earth which together become the one "home of God [which] is among mortals."

He will dwell with them as their God; they will be his peoples, and God himself will be with them; he will wipe every tear from their eyes. Death will be no more; mourning and crying and pain will be no more, for the first things have passed away. (Revelation 21:3,4)

The eschatological house of God which is the new heaven and new earth is a place filled with God's presence. It is a place where God's people will no longer weep, mourn, or suffer, for there will be no more pain. The host, God, will be the hospitable Presence who will wipe every tear from eyes long used to crying, and death itself will be defeated by God. Multitudes of voices will thunder hallelujahs to God, rejoicing and exulting in worship and praise to the Lamb slain and risen.

When we look at these biblical pictures of hospitality divine and human, we see that the resurrection stands at beginning and end as a kind of metaphorical bookends. At the beginning of the Christian journey stands conversion and baptism, death to life lived outside God's house and resurrection to life within God's world house and otherworld house, imaged by the waters of baptism and the words spoken to the baptizand. Upon emergence from the baptismal waters, the new Christian, resurrected to new Christ-life, moves to the Lord's Table and takes the bread and wine, body and blood, of Christ. From thence follows the Christian journey of discipleship.

Let us return to McClendon's practices model and develop it in light of what we have discovered from the biblical pictures. The formative practice of baptism, imaging death and resurrection, proceeds to the formative practice of Lord's Supper and its correlative transformative practice of discipleship and ministry. Resurrection proceeds directly to the Lord's Table, the centered matrix of hospitality, and thence to deeds and words of hospitality in a life journey of discipleship and ministry.

McClendon models this procession in the liturgy of his fictional (but true) Koinonia Church (McClendon, 1994:409–411). Baptism occurs early in the worship service following a time of preparation for worship, and the baptized ones proceed immediately to the Lord's Table and from there to their work of discipleship and ministry. This narrative progression follows that of the Christian journey or story itself. Ingredient to the entire narrative flow is "this is that" and a manner of reading scripture which McClendon describes in his *Ethics* and *Doctrine* as a foreshortened sense of future time.

What McClendon does not fully develop is what I am offering in this volume—the role of interlacing in this narrative progression. All the way along, the Christian disciple and minister interlaces the biblical stories of Jesus' baptism, the Last Supper in the upper room, the parable of the Last Judgment, the stories Jesus and his band of disciples live, and the many narratives Jesus tells in his own journey of ministry. In addition, the Christian and the faith community itself interlace a plethora of stories with the biblical stories at each post on the journey. Through it all, the norm for interpreting these many interlaced narratives remains the centrality of Jesus Christ and the resurrection.

Let us now return to Dinesen's narrative, *Babette's Feast*, itself a narrative of famine and feast, as well as of death, resurrection, and hospitality. It is not too much, I believe, to say that this, too, is a "Lord's Supper" or "Last Supper" narrative, and Babette is herself, as we have already seen, a figure of Christ. As earlier in this work, I believe that interlacing Dinesen's story with biblical and congregational narratives can add to the latter two true richness of depth as yet unreached; fine and precise, though understated, detail; and fresh, surprising nuance. Together the biblical, congregational, and literary narratives can render the complex, wondrous mystery of God in Christ and Christ in us, the people of God, in new, even astonishing, dimensions.

For Babette, the girded Jesus with towel and basin becomes the central christic image, gathering up into that image all her earlier ministrations, even as this servant image gathers up all Jesus' earlier ministry up to the kairotic moment of the upper room supper at Passover. Babette never appears in the banqueting room, but her self-sacrificial labors are present in the form of the inimitable cuisine which she instructs her youthful attendant to set before her guests. In the church's observance of the Lord's Supper, Jesus never appears in the supper room, but his self-expending labors and ministry are represented in the bread and cup. Babette, like Jesus, has poured out her great genius and spent all she is and has for this one purpose. All who dine at Babette's table, like all who dine at the Lord's Table, are transformed by the divine-human gift poured out upon them. Injuries among the Brotherhood are forgiven and relationships restored. Joy and blessing are given new birth. Jaded lives are revivified and each celebrant departs the table to love and serve and heal.

And something else—surpassingly deep and true—happens. I had lived with Dinesen's extraordinary story two years before I saw it! I had read and reread and read yet again *Babette's Feast*; I had lived with it, eating, working, and sleeping, for two years while I labored on this work. Still, I almost did not see it—this extraordinarily profound thing which Isak Dinesen sees and immortalizes in her splendid narrative. Once again, Dinesen's marvelous genius for understatement, the subtle nuance, the trembling image almost missed, bears both credit and responsibility.

To reveal my discovery, I need to focus the reader's gaze on the character of General Lorens Loewenhielm. Perhaps Dinesen keeps Babette out of the dining room, and thus out of the general's presence, so that her reader will focus also, soon or late, on this seemingly minor but very important character. Or perhaps Babette and the general never look upon each other and never speak because *their story's torque will not bear it.*

The story needs to be picked up in section VIII, "The Hymn." "Old Mrs. Loewenhielm" responds to Martine's and Philippa's dinner invitation with a note. Dinesen describes its content:

> Now, she wrote, her nephew, General Lorens Loewenhielm, had unexpectedly come on a visit; he had spoken with deep veneration of the Dean, and she begged permission to bring him with her. It would do him good, for the dear boy seemed to be in somewhat low spirits (Dinesen, 1953/1988:28).

Martine and Philippa write back to tell Mrs. Loewenhielm that they will be happy to welcome the general. And they tell Babette.

> They also called in Babette to inform her that *they would now be twelve* for dinner; they added that their latest guest had lived in Paris for several years. Babette seemed pleased with the news, and assured them that there would be food enough. (Dinesen, 1953/1988:28, emphasis added)

Now, let us move to section IX, "General Loewenhielm." Dinesen shows us a disquieted, pensive figure. He leads a "busy life at Court," spending much of his time at "the Tuileries and the Winter Palace." Obviously, the General is on the inside of things. But he is not happy. Indeed, he is a deeply troubled man. He has come home to his aunt's house to make an accounting of his life; "he was, as his aunt had written, in low spirits" (Dinesen, 1953/1988:31).

> General Loewenhielm had obtained everything that he had striven for in life. . . . He was in high favor with royalty . . . loyal to his king . . . an example to everybody. (Dinesen, 1953/1988:32)

But he has come to Fossum to "make out the balance-sheet of his life." Dinesen's religious allusion is apparent:

> Can the sum of a row of victories in many years and in many countries be a defeat? General Loewenhielm had fulfilled Lieutenant Loewenhielm's wishes and had more than satisfied his ambitions. *It might be held that he had gained the whole world.* And it had come to this, that the stately, worldly-wise older man now turned toward the naive young figure to ask him, gravely, even *bitterly, in what he had profited?* Somewhere *something had been lost.* (Dinesen, 1953/1988:33, emphasis added)

Dinesen seems to suggest that the young Lieutenant Loewenhielm became, over the course of his life, like the rich young ruler in Jesus' parable; and that he, like the biblical character, had as General Loewenhielm gained the whole world but lost his own soul. As the twelfth member among the invited table companions, *is he also compared by this magnificent and subtle storyteller to Judas Iscariot?* Let us continue to tease out Dinesen's meaning, for tease we must, because she will not tell us directly. At dinner, Babette gives explicit instructions to her attendant to pour only one glass of wine for the members of the Brotherhood but to refill the General's glass as often as he empties it. The award-winning film interpretation of *Babette's Feast* is in error when it suggests that the transformation wrought in the elderly women and men of the sect comes through intoxication from Babette's wine. Dinesen clearly tells her readers otherwise in the text; on this point, she leaves no doubt. What we almost lose, however, is the deeper meaning in Babette's instruction to her helper to fill the General's glass as soon as he empties it. It is unlikely that Babette's thought is solely and merely about the relative capacity of her guests to hold their liquor. In the sledge on the way to the dinner, General Loewenhielm had reminisced about a dinner given in his honor by dukes, French cavalry officers, and princes at the finest restaurant in Paris some years ago. Now, as the food is set before him, his mind goes back again to that dinner as he recognizes what he is being served: Amontillado, the best wine; turtle soup; Blinis Demidoff; Veuve Cliquot 1860, another of the finest French wines. What is General Loewenhielm beginning to realize? Here in a poor Lutheran household in Norway where, years before, he had been served cold haddock and a glass of water, he is now being served the finest cuisine, comparable to the best he has experienced. Let us look again at the text.

> General Loewenhielm stopped eating and sat immovable. Once more he was carried back to that dinner in Paris of which he had thought in the sledge. An incredibly recherche and palatable dish had been served there; he had asked its name from his fellow diner, *Colonel Gallifet*, and the Colonel had smilingly told him that it was named "Cailles en Sarcophage." He had further told him that the dish had been invented by the Chef of the very café in which they were dining, a person known all over Paris as the greatest culinary genius of the age, and—most surprisingly—a woman! "And indeed," said *Colonel Galliffet*, "this woman is now turning a dinner

146

at the Café Anglais into a kind of love affair—into a love affair of the noble and romantic category in which one no longer distinguishes between bodily and spiritual appetite or satiety! I have, before now, fought a duel for the sake of a fair lady. For no woman in all Paris, my young friend, would I more willingly shed my blood! (Dinesen, 1953/1988:38, emphasis added)

Like J and the best of the Hebrew storytellers, Dinesen leaves so vastly much unsaid. What else was the General thinking when he stopped eating and "sat immovable"? Surely not just about the superlative food, or even just about Colonel Galliffet and their conversation so many years ago. Does not his mind travel on to other turnings in the story, to other unfoldings of his and this renowned chef's narrative? How could this poor Norwegian house be now serving its guests what others have, heretofore, been privileged to dine upon only at the best restaurant in Paris?! From whence comes such *unparalleled hospitality*? And is it not unparalleled hospitality? In what other ways besides exquisite food and drink is it so? *What else* is this disillusioned, weary General being served this holy night? Is it not foolish to imagine that he still does not know who is beyond the door in the kitchen? What else does the General know which he and Dinesen are not telling us? *What more* has Babette served General Loewenhielm besides unlimited refills of exquisite and priceless French wine and incomparable French cuisine which he has savored nowhere else than at the Café Anglais, and not for many years?

What *sacrificial hospitality has Babette, girded with towel and bearing her servant's basin, placed before the General this sacred night*? We must hear his speech again.

Then the General felt that the time had come to make a speech. He rose and stood up very straight. "Mercy and truth, my friends, have met together," said the General. "Righteousness and bliss shall kiss one another." He spoke in a clear voice which had been trained in drill grounds and had echoed sweetly in royal halls, and yet he was speaking in a manner so new to himself and so strangely moving that after his first sentence he had to make a pause. For he was in the habit of forming his speeches with care, conscious of his purpose, but here, in the midst of the Dean's simple congregation, it was as if the whole figure of General Loewenhielm, his breast covered with decorations, were but a mouthpiece for a message which meant to be brought forth. "Man, my friends," said General

Loewenhielm, "is frail and foolish. We have all of us been told that grace is to be found in the universe. But in our human foolishness and short-sightedness we imagine divine grace to be finite. For this reason we tremble . . . " Never till now had the General stated that he trembled; he was genuinely surprised and even shocked at hearing his own voice proclaim the fact. "We tremble before making our choice in life, and after having made it again tremble in fear of having chosen wrong. But the moment comes when our eyes are opened, and we see and realize that grace is infinite. Grace, my friends, demands nothing from us but that we shall await it with confidence and acknowledge it in gratitude. Grace, brothers, makes no conditions and singles out none of us in particular; *grace takes us all to its bosom and proclaims general amnesty.* See! that which we have chosen is given us, and that which we have refused is, also and at the same time, granted us abundantly. *For mercy and truth have met together*, and righteousness and bliss have kissed one another!" (Dinesen, 1953/1988:40,41, emphasis added)

Dinesen's description of the change in General Loewenhielm's manner and mode of speech signals a profound change within his psyche. He is able to let himself be seen as vulnerable; this is revealed in his acknowledgment that he, like others, has trembled over his choices and deeds. His manner of speech is new even to himself, and the carefully trained voice of the military officer and orator in royal halls becomes a voice of uncommon charisma and power able to move the heart of the speaker himself as well as his hearers, not to military action or monarchic intentions, as before, but to receptivity to the gift of unlimited grace, the content of "a message which was meant to be brought forth." The depressed general counting his illustrious history as vanity and loss who came wanly to Babette's table has been transformed into an eloquent, magnetic spokesperson of hope and gratitude. Is it too much to say that he has been resurrected? Can we imagine that this banquet table in the sisters' house has been for him a sacred communion table, offering a holy eucharist of bread and wine, a Lord's Supper experience of resurrection, for General Loewenhielm, as well as for others of his table companions? Dinesen herself seems to appraise it so. Her comments on her characters' experience at this graceful table seem even to harbor an implied allusion to the eschatological feast in Revelation. "The vain illusions of this earth had dissolved before their eyes like

148

smoke, and they had seen the universe as it really is. They had been given one hour of the millennium" (Dinesen, 1953/1988:42). Refusing to separate radically the sacred from the mundane, Dinesen evidently locates the Lord's Table not just in the sanctuary but in the dining room as well. Refusing also to dichotomize history into pre- and post-eschatological time, Dinesen locates the eschatological feast and the Great Supper of the Lamb slain and risen as both present and yet-to-be. McClendon's notion of foreshortened sense of future time is helpful for understanding what Dinesen is suggesting.

General Loewenhielm has experienced release from his burden. Might he have needed *forgiveness*, and this is what he has been granted? Has Babette's gift of culinary genius been also *a gift of forgiveness*? We shall need to follow the story farther to find out. As yet, we are uncertain what the General's need of forgiveness, if any, has been. And as we do not know what his sin has been, we do not know what restitution he has offered, what repentance he has made. Here, the character, only briefly mentioned, of Colonel Galliffet needs our attention. As we noted earlier, General Loewenhielm reminisces about a Colonel Galliffet as the fellow diner (his close friend?) at a long ago dinner given in his honor, a companion who first told him about the renowned woman chef whose incomparable dishes they were even then enjoying at the Café Anglais. This Colonel Galliffet is alone named among the princes, officers, and dukes present at that dinner. Why? Is it merely because Galliffet was the one who told Loewenhielm about the greatest chef in Paris? Dinesen could as easily have put that information in the mouth of one of the princes and dukes. Why Colonel Galliffet? How close is the relationship between Galliffet and Loewenhielm? Perhaps the single clue to an answer to this latter question is the seating arrangement at this honorary dinner and the fact that Loewenhielm himself mentally names only Galliffet's name among those in this illustrious party who were present to honor him.

Let us continue to tease out this lead. Where else does the storyteller put the name of Galliffet before her readers? Dinesen's powerful last scene needs again our full attention. She entitles it "The Great Artist":

When Martine and Philippa locked the door they remembered

149

Babette. A little wave of tenderness and pity swept through them: Babette alone had had no share in the bliss of the evening. So they went out into the kitchen, and Martine said to Babette: "It was quite a nice dinner, Babette."

Their hearts filled with gratitude. They realized that none of their guests had said a single word about the food. Indeed, try as they might, they could not themselves remember any of the dishes which had been served.

· ·

Babette sat on the chopping block, surrounded by more black and greasy pots and pans than her mistresses had ever seen in their life. She was as white and as deadly exhausted as on the night when she first appeared and had fainted on their doorstep.

After a long time she looked straight at them and said: "I was once cook at the Café Anglais."

Martine said again: "They all thought that it was a nice dinner." And when Babette did not answer a word she added: "We will all remember this evening when you have gone back to Paris, Babette."

Babette said: "I am not going back to Paris."

"You are not going back to Paris?" Martine exclaimed.

"No," said Babette. "What will I do in Paris? They have all gone. I have lost them all, Mesdames."

The sisters' thoughts went to Monsieur Hersant and his son, and they said: "Oh, my poor Babette."

"Yes, they have all gone," said Babette. "The Duke of Morny, the Duke of Decazes, Prince Narishkine, *General Galliffet*, Aurélian Scholl, Paul Daru, the Princesse Pauline! All!"

The strange names and titles of people lost to Babette faintly confused the two ladies, but there was such an infinite perspective of tragedy in her announcement that in their respective state of mind they felt her losses as their own, and their eyes filled with tears.

At the end of another long silence Babette suddenly smiled slightly at them and said: "And how would I go back to Paris, Mesdames? I have no money."

"No money?" the sisters cried as with one mouth.

"No," said Babette.

"But the ten thousand francs?" the sisters asked in a horrified gasp.

"The ten thousand francs have been spent, Mesdames," said Babette.

The sisters sat down. For a full minute they could not speak.

150

"But ten thousand francs?" Martine slowly whispered.

"What will you, Mesdames," said Babette with great dignity. "A dinner for twelve at the Café Anglais would cost ten thousand francs."

The ladies still did not find a word to say. The piece of news was incomprehensible to them, but then many things tonight in one way or another had been beyond comprehension.

. . . .

But Philippa's heart was melting in her bosom. It seemed *an unforgettable proof of human loyalty and self-sacrifice.*

"Dear Babette," she said softly, "you ought not to have given away all you had for our sake."

Babette gave her mistress a deep glance, a strange glance. Was there not pity, even scorn, at the bottom of it?

"For your sake?" she replied. "No. For my own."

She rose from the chopping block and stood up before the two sisters.

"I am a great artist!" she said. She waited a moment and then repeated: "I am a great artist, Mesdames."

Again for a long time there was a deep silence in the kitchen. Then Martine said: "So you will be poor now all your life, Babette?"

"Poor?" said Babette. She smiled as if to herself. "No, I shall never be poor. I told you that I am a great artist. A great artist, Mesdames, is never poor. We have something, Mesdames, of which other people know nothing."

While the elder sister found nothing more to say, in Philippa's heart deep, forgotten chords vibrated. For she had heard before now, long ago, of the Café Anglais. She had heard, before now, long ago, the names on Babette's tragic list. She rose and took a step toward her servant.

"But all those people whom you have mentioned," she said, "those princes and great people of Paris whom you named, Babette? You yourself fought against them. You were a Communard. *The General you named had your husband and son shot!* How can you grieve over them?"

Babette's dark eyes met Philippa's. "Yes," she said, "I was a Communard. Thanks be to God, I was a Communard! And those people whom I named, Mesdames, were evil and cruel. They let the people of Paris starve; they oppressed and wronged the poor. Thanks be to God. I stood upon a barricade; I loaded the gun for my menfolk! But all the same, Mesdames, I shall not go back to Paris, now that those people of whom I have spoken are no

151

longer there." She stood immovable, lost in thought. "You see, Mesdames," she said, at last, "those people belonged to me, they were mine. They had been brought up and trained, with greater expense than you, my little ladies, could ever imagine or believe, to understand what a great artist I am. I could make them happy. When I did my very best I could make them perfectly happy." (Dinesen, 1953/1988:44–48, emphasis added)

Here, in Babette's final speech (she has spoken but little throughout this story), Babette mentions a *General* Galliffet. Evidently, this is the same person as *Colonel* Galliffet whom General Loewenhielm remembers as his fellow diner many years ago. Unlike General Loewenhielm, however, who remembers by name only one of those patrons of the Café Anglais, Babette includes General Galliffet's name in a list of dukes, princes, and other members of royalty and the aristocracy. Their names and titles, after many years, are still fresh to her.

The reader, perhaps, is shocked to learn from Philippa that this General Galiffet is the commanding officer who ordered the execution of Babette's husband and son. Dinesen reminds her readers that Philippa had already heard the General's name many years ago. Thumbing back through the story, we find in Achille Papin's letter of recommendation of Babette to the sisters' employ what then seemed of minor importance for the further development of Dinesen's narrative:

The bearer of this letter, Madame Babette Hersant, like my beautiful Empress herself, has had to flee from Paris. Civil war has raged in our streets. French hands have shed French blood. The noble Communards, standing up for the Rights of Man, have been crushed and annihilated. Madame Hersant's husband and son, both eminent ladies' hairdressers, have been shot. She herself was arrested as a Petroleuse—(which word is used here for women who set fire to houses with petroleum)—and has narrowly escaped the blood-stained hands of *General Galliffet*. She has lost all she possessed and dares not remain in France. (Dinesen, 1953/1988:13)

Dinesen's terse narrative has put a Colonel/General Galliffet's name before her readers four times; once each, he has been mentioned by Achille Papin, General Loewenhielm, Babette, and Philippa. We know only that he was a member of a dinner party honoring the young Lieutenant Loewenhielm, that Loewenhielm named him alone among those at that table, that Galliffet admired

Babette's culinary genius and insinuated a romantic interest in her, and that he ordered the killing of her husband and son after the fall of the Communards and, evidently, ordered her execution, as well, though she escaped from France. Whether or not Galliffet is still alive, we do not know. But we do know that General Loewenhielm was closely associated with him.

Teasing out Dinesen's provocative leads is risky. Are we making General Loewenhielm guilty by association? Nowhere does he mention the Paris Commune in his dinner table repartee. Yet his friend, Colonel Galliffet, evidently became General Galliffet who ordered the political execution of the Hersant's after the fall of the resistance. Where was General Loewenhielm during this bloody time in France's history and struggle? Dinesen never tells us—directly. Yet she does tell us that, in his bright uniform, General Loewenhielm "strutted and shone like an ornamental bird," his chest "covered with decorations" (Dinesen, 1953/1988:30). And we learn that he enjoys favor at court, spends much of his time there, is loyal to the king, and is respected by all.

Can it be that General Loewenhielm has received at Babette Hersant's banquet table what he has needed most, a gift transfiguring enough to transform his melancholy accounting of his life as a defeat, a mocking, paradoxical "sum of a row of victories in many years and in many countries"? *Has General Loewenhielm been granted forgiveness at Babette's communion table*? Is he now released from a long-carried burden of guilt? Is this why he speaks (as he has never spoken before with all his training and experience) with uncommon eloquence on the subject of grace? He alone names the dinner party's mutual experience as one of grace. All the communicants, it appears, with the possible exception of Martine and Philippa, have forgiven and been forgiven.

It would seem that Babette Hersant and General Loewenhielm have given and received forgiveness without ever seeing or speaking to each other. With the giving of art, gift, self, and hospitality and their reception with full appreciation, there has transpired between these two persons the mutual giving and receiving of respect, the content of love. General Loewenhielm has been the only person at Babette's feast able to receive fully her gift of self and art. Repeatedly, he exclaims his amazement and pleasure to his taciturn fellow diners, though without reciprocation, and, slowly, he comes to realize who is in the kitchen—the most celebrated culinary genius of her day, Babette Hersant. The fact that he does not request to see her and speak to her lends added weight to the interpretation I am offering. Their story's tragic reality is the reason. He knows that she has again expended her great genius for his pleasure despite the history they have lived; *His feet have been washed.*

Even General Galliffet has been forgiven. How else can we explain Babette's speaking his name in her list of those "who were mine"? Without his and their presence in Paris, she will now decline the opportunity to return to her beloved city, the city where she reigned as the supreme culinary genius of her day.

Babette's hospitality has transformed the sisters' house into a prototype of God's world house. Dinesen's short story is an extended parable, shocking us with its reversal of our expectations. As John Dominic Crossan and Sallie McFague have pointed out regarding the dynamic power of parabolic narrative, this story shatters our structures of expectation, breaking them open, and giving God's Spirit room to work (Crossan, 1975, and McFague, 1975). What we expected to happen does not happen. What happens does not fit our expectations. Can it be that the gentle and loving Martine and Philippa are, of all those at Babette's feast this sacred evening, the ones least able to receive her gift of grace? Let us look again at their response to the banquet and what has transpired among their table companions.

Philippa and Martine believe that Babette has "had no share in the bliss of the evening." How obtuse! Indeed, as Dinesen reveals, Babette's bliss has *exceeded* that of her guests; once more, she has had the opportunity to do her best. For all the years of Babette's service to the sisters, Martine and Philippa had not permitted Babette to do even her second-best. Upon her arrival in their household, they had given her strict instructions regarding how to prepare their simple food and had never sought her ideas or contributions. The austerity of their home and its rejection of earthly pleasures had forced Babette to deny her genius and had accorded her no opportunity to express it.

Now, after this sumptuous feast, Martine and Philippa cannot even remember what they have eaten, and the best commendation they have to offer is, "It was quite a nice dinner, Babette."

On this holy evening, Babette has girded herself with towel

and basin, but Martine and Philippa have not plunged their feet into the water. Like Simon Peter's response to Jesus, theirs also has been, "You shall not wash my feet." The sisters, feet drawn back from the waiting basin, do not understand Babette's extravagantly generous expenditure of ten thousand francs (all that she has), and cannot fathom and appropriate Babette's attitude toward her enemies. Martine and Philippa are good people, caring gently and sacrificially for the needs of their community, those whom they cherish as friend and beloved. But they are unable to understand Babette's respectful cherishing of those who killed her husband and son. For Martine and Philippa, one cannot ambiguously be both friend and enemy, both appreciatively loved and strenuously opposed. In their true though limited way, they have lived the Christian story, but they have never entered its deepest narrative as Babette has done. For them, the enemy remains the enemy.

Still, though Martine and Philippa have forfeited much of goodness and grace, General Loewenhielm is right; the nature of grace is such that even that which has been rejected is given again. The final scene between Philippa and Babette extends grace and hospitality forward into the day yet to come beyond this hallowed evening.

In her youth Philippa had rejected the gift of her own inimitable voice and the pleasure and comfort it might have given to others, rich and poor. She, like Babette, possessed a great art and was, though quiescent and undeveloped, a great artist. Had she exercised the courage to act on Achille Papin's encouragement, Philippa might in time have said with Babette: "I could make them happy. When I did my very best I could make them perfectly happy." Let us pick up the story after Babette's assertion:

> She paused for a moment.
> "It was like that with Monsieur Papin too," she said.
> "With Monsieur Papin?" Philippa asked.
> "Yes, with your Monsieur Papin, my poor lady," said Babette. "He told me so himself: 'It is terrible and unbearable to an artist,' he said, 'to be encouraged to do, to be applauded for doing, his second best.' He said: 'Through all the world there goes one long cry from the heart of the artist: Give me leave to do my utmost!'"
> Philippa went up to Babette and put her arms around her. She felt the cook's body like a marble monument against her

own, but she herself shook and trembled from head to foot. For a while she could not speak. Then she whispered:

"Yet this is not the end! I feel, Babette, that this is not the end. In Paradise you will be the great artist that God meant you to be! Ah!" she added, the tears streaming down her cheeks. "Ah, how you will enchant the angels!" (Dinesen, 1953/1988:48)

Philippa's tears are for herself. But they are not tears just of remorse and regret for what has been lost. They are tears also of thanksgiving for what can still be. Dinesen's story is not finally a story of gifts wasted and opportunities forfeited, but a story of grace and hospitality, wherein the line between this world and the next is permeable and translucent. Babette's feast is at once a last supper and an eschatological foretaste of what is to come.

Dinesen both writes and interprets her story in light of the Jesus story. Like the Last Supper in the Christian story, Babette's supper does not end there, but is extended forward in the Lord's Supper in the Christian congregation where forgiveness is offered and received in every new day. For that reason, these Christian women who have rejected much of God's graciousness to them can yet receive what is always and everywhere being offered to them time and again. As I stated earlier, Dinesen does not disjoin the Lord's Table in the sanctuary from the Lord's Table in the dining room. Grace has been poured forth through food and drink at Babette's table, and grace is poured forth through the Christ-like person of Babette herself. Whether in the sanctuary or in the sisters' humble dining room, the Lord's Table is spread for penitent Christians ready to receive God's abundant hospitality.

Just as Dinesen does not absolutely separate the Lord's Table in sanctuary and in dining room, she also does not separate absolutely present and future time. A foreshortened sense of future time informs her perspective, and a mystical, aesthetic view of reality collapses radical, impermeable boundaries between present history and eschatological future. I am reminded of the film a few years ago entitled *Field of Dreams* wherein characters traveled freely from the hereafter back into the present and communicated with those still enclosed in history. While Dinesen's idea is not exactly the same, both *Field of Dreams* and *Babette's Feast* offer another perspective on the ancient church doctrine of the communion of saints. In a sermon preached on All Saint's Day a few years ago, Mel Williams talked about our "balcony people," those Christian saints who have gone on ahead of us but who are up there in the balcony cheering us on as we continue the saintly struggle here in this space-time continuum. Mel's suggestion connects with Dinesen's and the ecclesiological tradition itself; communion among the saints "over there" and those still here happens, though on a level beyond our full comprehension.

Philippa's and Martine's story, like that of the other characters in Dinesen's wonderful narrative, is one of hope. The door of God's world house and otherworld house remains open to them, as to all others. Again, it seems paradoxical that we would need to say and hear this word of reassurance about these good women, but they, more than the other characters in this tale, have resisted the hospitality offered them. Thus, it is their future about which we have some uneasiness. We sense that the General and the elderly brothers and sisters have experienced true resurrection to a life of forgiveness and restored joy. So, too, Babette, we know from her own mouth, will never be poor. She has spent her gifts fully—unselfishly, hospitably, and christically.

Before leaving *Babette's Feast* and as re-introduction to the biblical narratives, I want to return our attention to General Loewenhielm's experience of grace and forgiveness in the context of Babette's hospitality. Let us backtrack to the time of preparation for the anniversary dinner when Babette learns that General Loewenhielm will be the twelfth member of the dinner party. She remembers him and knows his connection to General Galliffet and the violent events of the insurrection. She, doubtless, knows the extent to which he participated in the crushing of the resistance and the role he played in her own tragic losses. She knows, too, that he will be the only guest at her table who will be capable of appreciating her genius. She does her best *for him*. Pouring out her art and strength at great personal and financial expense to herself, she makes him happy. The extent of Babette's sacrifice is implied in Dinesen's description of her character after the guests have left, beatifically cavorting and laughing and blessing one another.

> "She was as white and as deadly exhausted as on the night when she first appeared and had fainted on their doorstep." (Dinesen, 1953/1988:44)

157

We are reminded that Babette was fleeing for her life on that night long ago. On this night, she has poured out her life's energy and genius for one who was among those who sought her life. *For her enemy she has sacrificed herself.* He is a cherished enemy. He is also her kindred spirit, a friend. She will not, cannot, radically disjoin the two.

Dinesen's story invites careful reflection on the intrinsic connection which holds in creative-redemptive tension, hospitality, forgiveness, and resurrection. In the context and setting of hospitality, the giving and receiving of forgiveness are enabled and resurrection occurs. The enemy becomes a *cherished enemy.* Enemy still, one who in some measure must still be opposed, he or she is now a cherished enemy.

Interlacing *Babette's Feast* with biblical narratives of Jesus' interaction with persons needing forgiveness and restoration illumines the hospitable setting in which reconciliation happens. Jesus constructs a setting of hospitality, or he and they together, in some instances, construct this setting. Pouring his genius and energy out upon these needy ones, relating in a hospitable manner to them, Jesus restores them and they experience forgiveness and transformation.

The central example of Jesus' transformative interaction with the cherished enemy is his blessing spoken from the cross. Before we look directly, however, at that central image and event, let us look at other stories of forgiveness given and received in hospitality. The story of the woman taken in adultery, in the eighth chapter of John, attracts our examination. In the hospitable context of teacher and learners at the temple, Jesus opens a space for the adulterous woman brought before him. Discerning the inhospitable and devious motive behind the scribes' and pharisees' action in dragging this woman before him for judgment, Jesus quietly slows down the pace as he kneels silently and writes on the ground. Twice he does this, once as they await his adjudication, and again as the accusers file singly away when they know they, too, have unrepented and unforgiven sins. Quietly and confidently, Jesus changes the hostile setting to one which now is a part of God's hospitable world house. Here, there is gracious room for her, too. She is empowered toward metanoia; now, she can turn away from her self-destructive sin, receive forgiveness, and be resurrected from death to new life.

Rembrandt interpreted this biblical story artistically through the medium of painting and, for those who have seen his remarkable painting or a reproduction of it, reshuffled their perceptions dramatically. Rembrandt's interpretation sheds new light on the power and dimensions of Jesus' hospitality and its transformative effect on this unfortunate woman. To the viewer's surprise, Rembrandt paints her as young, lovely, exquisitely gowned in white, her dainty blue slippers matched by a blue sash around her waist, and her golden hair intricately and beautifully coiffed. Although she is kneeling before Jesus, she has the aspect of a queen kneeling before a king. Was Rembrandt saying that Jesus' transformative hospitality and loving respect were such that now she could be this person? That is how I interpret this outstanding artist's timeless work; is it not Christologically genuine?

A similar transformation and resurrection occur for the Samaritan woman. After five husbands and now a sixth man who might soon leave her, this woman has cause to need a restoration of hope. As she approaches the well where a tired and thirsty Jesus sits, Jesus begins to mold a setting of hospitality. This he does principally by speaking to her; additionally, by engaging her in conversation. Having so extended hospitality, now by requesting a cup of water, Jesus dependently places himself in the position of one needing and willing to receive hospitality from her. Reciprocally giving and receiving hospitality, Jesus and the Samaritan woman enlarge their context of hospitality with interactive dialogue which moves her, like the woman in John's narrative, to repentance, forgiveness, hope, and renewal.

Another woman transformed by Jesus' amazing ability to create a setting of hospitality in the center of hostility is the distraught woman who intrudes herself at Simon the Pharisee's house. Desperate for forgiveness and renewal, she herself initiates with Jesus a fascinating and intricately-interweaving game of hospitable give-and-take at Simon's dinner party. We need to look directly at Luke's narrative and follow its interesting progression:

> One of the pharisees asked Jesus to eat with him, and he went into the Pharisee's house and took his place at the table. And a woman in the city, who was a sinner, having learned that he was eating in the Pharisee's house, brought an alabaster jar of ointment. She stood behind him at his feet, weeping, and began to

bathe his feet with her tears and to dry them with her hair. Then she continued kissing his feet and anointing them with the ointment. Now when the Pharisee who had invited him saw it, he said to himself, "If this man were a prophet, he would have known who is touching him—that she is a sinner."

Jesus spoke up and said to him, "Simon I have something to say to you." "Teacher," he replied, "Speak." "A certain creditor had two debtors; one owed five hundred denarii, and the other fifty. When they could not pay, he canceled the debts for both of them. Now which of them will love him more?" Simon answered, "I suppose the one for whom he canceled the greater debt." And Jesus said to him, "You have judged rightly." Then turning toward the woman, he said to Simon, "Do you see this woman? I entered your house; you gave me no water for my feet, but she has bathed my feet with her tears and dried them with her hair. You gave me no kiss, but from the time I came in she has not stopped kissing my feet. You did not anoint my head with oil, but she has anointed my feet with ointment. Therefore, I tell you, her sins, which were many, have been forgiven, hence she has shown great love. But the one to whom little is forgiven, loves little." Then he said to her, "Your sins are forgiven."

But those who were at the table with him began to say among themselves, "Who is this who even forgives sins?" And he said to the woman, "Your faith has saved you; go in peace." (Luke 7:36–50)

This story begins with an invitation to dinner. A Pharisee named Simon issues an ostensibly hospitable invitation to Jesus to have dinner at his house. Soon after Jesus takes his place at the table, a woman "who was a sinner" enters with an alabaster jar of costly ointment. How she gains entry and manages not to be forthwith ejected we are not told. However that is, she begins washing Jesus' dusty feet not with water but with her tears and drying them not with a towel but with her hair. As if this were not extravagant enough, she now kisses not his head or hands but his feet repeatedly and anoints not his head with oil but, again, his feet. Simon, the host, is offended by the woman's unseemly behavior and Jesus' apparently ignorant and politically unwise acceptance of it. Jesus knows that Simon disapproves of all he witnesses and addresses his host directly, telling him a story about a creditor who forgave two debtors, one a great sum and the other a tenth that amount. Jesus connects forgiveness and love and signifies direct correspondence between the two. Having laid the groundwork for what he intends to say more directly, *Jesus explicitly identifies the central issue at stake as one of hospitality* and its relation to forgiveness, love, and restoration. Simon has withheld hospitality from his invited guest. The uninvited sinful woman, however, has lavished hospitality on another's slighted guest.

> I entered your house; you gave me no water for my feet, but she has bathed my feet with her tears and dried them with her hair. You gave me no kiss, but from the time I came in she has not stopped kissing my feet. You did not anoint my head with oil, but she has anointed my feet with ointment. (Luke 7:44b-46)

Simon has withheld the customary amenities a host is expected to extend his guest—water for his feet, a kiss of welcome, and anointing with oil. He has extended no hospitality to Jesus, but on the contrary, by withholding customary acts of hospitality, has insulted his guest. The sinful woman, on the other hand, who owed no deeds of hospitality to Jesus, has extravagantly created a setting of hospitality without equal.

Jesus concludes his reprimand to Simon by revealing the seriousness of his omissions. By refusing hospitality, Simon has further hardened his own heart, making it virtually impermeable to forgiveness. At this point, Jesus' words describe a dynamic interplay of hospitality, repentance, love, and forgiveness which admits of no simple progression from one to the other as from A to B to C to D. Rather, a complex interplay of hospitable attitudes and acts, contrition and repentance, feelings and intentions of love, and forgiveness and freedom, resists any reductionistic effort to simplify the process. Has the woman loved first, or been forgiven first? It is not easy to tell. Is it because she has loved so greatly and poured out such effusive hospitality that she is now forgiven? Or is it because she sinned so greatly and has been forgiven so much that now she expresses her gratitude with such love and generous hospitality? Does Jesus suggest that Simon loves little because his sins are fewer and his need of forgiveness less weighty than hers? Although that might seem to be the conclusion if one reads Jesus' parable superficially, such a reading does not comport with what we already know about Jesus' estimation of the gravity of the sin of the pharisees and scribes.

Let me reiterate an earlier observation. By refusing to relate with hospitality, Simon hardens his heart, steeling it against recognition of his sin and contrite repentance. Therefore, he is forgiven little. It is not that Simon's record has few sins on it or that Jesus is unwilling to forgive his sin. Rather, it is Simon who draws the terms. Withholding the water, kiss, and oil of hospitality, Simon constricts his heart and renounces his opportunity for forgiveness and freedom. The woman, on the other hand, withholds nothing of hospitality nor of repentance. Her many sins are forgiven.

> "Therefore, I tell you, her sins, which were many, have been forgiven; hence she has shown great love. But the one to whom little is forgiven, loves little." Then he said to her, "Your sins are forgiven." But those who were at the table with him began to say among themselves, "Who is this who even forgives sins?" And he said to the woman, "Your faith has saved you; go in peace." (Luke 7:47-50)

Jesus simply states that her sins *are* forgiven. At what point in time did the forgiveness happen? Again, this is unclear, and it is risky to try to define the interplay in terms of progression from one point to the next. Her faith which has saved her and now permits her to go in peace is a rich, interlaced fabric of trust, love, hospitality, respect mutually given and received, contrition, and repentance. It is this complex divine-human weave which grants her forgiveness and peace, liberation and joy.

One final observation needs to be made about this story of hospitality. Jesus becomes both recipient of hospitality and giver of hospitality. (Perhaps hospitality must always be reciprocally expressed to be what it is). He does not reject the woman's offerings but hospitably opens a space of mutual respect for the two of them. He respects her gifts and receives them gratefully. She respects him in like manner. She has needed the acceptance and forgiveness he gives her; he has needed the trust and respect she gives him. The dance of hospitality in their relating is of the stuff of eternity, the content of God's world house and otherworld house. Together, in Simon's inhospitable room, Jesus and the woman create a space of hospitality which partakes of the reality of God's house here and in the beyond.

Jesus relates graciously and hospitably to the people in his world not merely for kindness' sake but because he knows *that the hospitable context as prototype of God's house is the formative setting participating in the narrative movement from death to life.*

Superimposing biblical picture upon picture, we have seen that hospitality, forgiveness, hope, renewal, and resurrection co-inhere in the scriptural narratives. Interlacing *Babette's Feast* and biblical pictorial stories, we have discovered the nature of God's world house and otherworld house as a house of hospitality where mutual respect is given and received, gifts are expressed and appreciated, and forgiveness, restoration, and joy transform stories of death into stories of resurrection.

Now, let us return to the theme of the cherished enemy and the story of the cross. While Dinesen's remarkable story and its uncommon valuation of the enemy as one who also is close to us shines valuable light on the biblical narratives, it has first drawn its own light and inspiration from the scriptural source. This fact is made evidently clear by Dinesen's many religious allusions. At places, she virtually lifts scriptural phrases directly from the text and transposes them into her own. Thus, Babette is a Christ figure who can respect and care for the one(s) who have sought to kill her. Dinesen's preference for understatement and allusion prevent her naming the passion story as her primary source for molding Babette as such a figure, but it has unmistakably served as her model and impetus.

Jesus has now spun the red thread of self-sacrifice fully.

> And when they came to the place which is called The Skull, there they crucified him, and the criminals, one on the right and one on the left. And Jesus said, "Father, forgive them; for they know not what they do." And they cast lots to divide his garments. (Luke 23:33,34, RSV)

Though his persecutors and executioners have neither sought forgiveness nor opened their hearts to receive it, Jesus prays for their delivery. They are still his own. They share the human condition with him, with all its hardship and tears, its backbreaking labor and shattered dreams. At one point, they cheered him on, sought healing for their diseases, and liberation for their people, and looked to him to provide it or give them leadership in achieving it. They recognized his genius and appreciated it. He was the greatest figure of their day. But now they have turned against him. Political tides have washed over them all and threatened to sweep everything away with them. Now, they wish to destroy him and return things to their former condition. Jesus knows all this, and he knows that these who are his enemies remain the enemy, but they are a cherished enemy. They are the ones for whom he has poured out his great genius and now shed his blood itself. Holding wide the doors of God's world house and otherworld house with outstretched, cruciform arms, Jesus respects, loves, and forgives. They have made themselves the enemy, but they are the *cherished enemy*. He will not let them go. He will yet offer the hospitality of God's own house and bid them enter. Doing so, Jesus moves toward his own resurrection and theirs, the new day dawning, marked by hope, renewal and victory over all manner of death, over all that would hold in the pit of the grave those whom God cherishes.

Narrative Ecclesiology: Church and Story

The nature and mission of the church rest on the person, work, authority, and commission of Jesus Christ. Classically, theologians of the church have defined the church in terms of four predicates: one, holy, apostolic, and catholic. Those guiding images have served the church in understanding itself and its work. In some periods of history threats to the integrity of the church have been met and countered by the guiding conviction of unity. At other times, challenges to doctrinal orthodoxy and faithfulness to Jesus Christ have been successfully met by the defining predicate of holiness. Other efforts to subvert the church's mission and distort its identity have been defeated by the church's self-definition in terms of apostolicity. Similarly, catholicity has clarified for the church its relation and mission to the world.

The church as one, holy, apostolic, and catholic still has value for ecclesiological identity and understanding. However, contemporary narrative ecclesiology focuses on other images of the church not traditionally emphasized so strongly as those classical ones. Less developed images of church including those of pilgrims, people of God, household of faith, and peacemakers claim biblical origination and warranty alongside the better known ones, and narrativists are turning now to those biblical images in reconstructing the doctrine of the church.

Still, merely reaching into a grab-bag of images is hardly the way to go about the important task of developing a doctrine of the church, and the church has never taken that kind of insincere approach. Rather, questions about the central issues of ecclesiology are asked and considered. Dietrich Bonhoeffer phrased the question, "Who is Jesus Christ for us today?" (Bonhoeffer, 1953/1979:279). As we labor to answer faithfully that central question, we can then also begin to answer the question, How can the church be the church today? Bonhoeffer's own answer to the ecclesiological question, which depended on his answer to the Christological one, asserted the church's identity as a radical fellowship of the cross. Cheap grace would not admit entry into that fellowship; only costly grace would suffice (Bonhoeffer, 1954;1937/1961;1953/1979). Now, we need to ask, what do those terms, "radical fellowship of the cross," "cheap grace," and "costly grace" mean at the end of this second Christian millennium?

Narrative ecclesiology attempts to offer an answer by fashioning a Christologically and biblically-shaped vision and construction. Biblical pictures and narratives are interlaced with narratives and pictures of worship and discipleship from the congregation itself and with pictures from biography and the literary, visual, and performing arts. Other stories from other sources offer rich material for the theological task, as well. When those multitudinous pictures and narratives are assembled, resurrection images rise to the top of the pool. Jesus' resurrection, ours, and the resurrection life of the church we then identify as the centerpiece of both ecclesiology and discipleship. Anastatic life proleptically fleshed out in the here and now with gaze fastened on the horizon of God's new heaven and new earth stands at the midpoint. All else arranges itself around that pivot. Accordingly, I wish to focus on Paul's conception of the resurrection body as a spiritual body, stated in I Corinthians 15.

Perhaps it is not particularly theologically presumptuous to speculate on what a spiritual body might mean for the church and for Christians today. At the least, Paul's arcane notion seems to signify an unwillingness to separate body and spirit dualistically and to draw an impermeable line between earth and heaven. I would suggest that the resurrection church living already in the anastatic realm manifests its spiritual body as it lives its gospel narrative in the here and now in concrete relation to also here and now realities of exclusion, hate, greed, violence, ecological plunder, and homophobia. This last issue is perhaps the most difficult and most intransigent one of all. It would seem that Christians and Christian churches can welcome to God's hospitality table the poor, the diseased (except for those with AIDS sexually contracted), even blacks and other racial and ethnic minorities. But homosexual men and women are a rejected and excluded class unto themselves. Unless they deny their sexual and relational needs and live celibate lives, gay men and lesbian women place themselves, the common opinion holds, beyond the pale of God's grace.

It is time now that Christian theologians and ethicists speak forthrightly to this issue, even as Letty Russell has done in her latest book, *Church in the Round*. We have much hard work to do. The findings of the biological sciences, psychology, and sociology and the stories homosexual women and men live and tell, insights from the arts and wisdom from the humanities, everything the church can find to help it to open its ears, to hear, to strive to understand, and to engage in respectful dialogue with those who suffer this harshest of ostracisms need careful examination and attention. The responsible work certain Christian groups have already done can facilitate this task. The findings of the World Council of Churches study commissions, the experience of Presbyterian More Light congregations, that of MCC churches, and the discoveries of individual Christian congregations like Pullen Memorial Baptist Church in Raleigh, North Carolina can enable this important investigation. Many voices need to be expressed and heard as the church struggles its way toward faithfulness in relation to homosexual persons and the meaning of God's hospitality for them.

Resurrected to hospitality, the church, with its author Jesus Christ, joins his work of opening the doors to God's house and inviting all to enter. The church practice which most clearly signifies that resurrection nature is the formative practice of the Eucharist or Lord's Supper. As a Table Community resurrected to hospitality, the church is both spirit and body, body and spirit; in Paul's words, it is a *spiritual body*. There is an intrinsic link between the event of resurrection and the sacrament of the Lord's Supper's retelling and reenacting the event itself in the worship and discipleship of the church. All are invited to the table as all are invited into the divine household. Table companions partake together bread and wine signifying the body and blood of Jesus himself and become in spirit and body those who continue to live his life and story in the world.

In the *Church Dogmatics*, Karl Barth named the church as the "earthly-historical form of the existence of Jesus Christ" (Barth, 1956). This *"irdisch-geschichtlichen"* form of Jesus' own life which is the Christian community will rightfully then, I believe, constitute itself as a life of hospitality oriented and focused in the same way as Jesus' life of ministry and self-sacrifice. Post-resurrection life is what Barth is describing in the *Dogmatics*, post-resurrection life for both Jesus and the church which is now his earthly-historical existence. In my dissertation study published by Scholars Press under the title *An Affront to the Gospel? The Radical Barth and the Southern Baptist Convention*, I set forth the thesis that, informed by this conception of Barth's, we see that the church's nature and tasks have principally to do with spiritual salvation *and* social-ecological restoration, one nature and task with both spiritual and bodily dimensions (Barnes, 1987).

Now, I wish to expand that thesis by pointing out that the resurrection church as earthly-historical form of the existence of Jesus Christ manifests its spiritual body by its faithfulness to the narrative Jesus lived from Nazareth to Golgotha. This means that living that redemptive plot as modern-day characters in the grand Gospel story, the church and Christians who constitute the Body of Christ enflesh and enact a story of salvation, peace, ecojustice, and hospitality. As a congregation of table companions, the church knows itself to be the people of God, pilgrims, narrative journeyers, a household of faith on the way. As Jesus is the Prince of Peace, the church is peopled by peacemakers on journey. As Jesus is the Bread of Life and the Vine, at the Table of the Lord's Supper the church partakes of bread and wine, natural elements of the ecosystem with ecojustice implications. As Jesus is Cornerstone and Door, the church is the Household of God. As Jesus is Light, the church in continuing incarnation is light to the world. As Jesus is the Way, Christians are people of the Way on narrative journey with him. All of this has meaning for the radical fellowship of the cross and costly grace whereof Bonhoeffer speaks.

Classical apprehensions of the church as one, holy, apostolic, and catholic depend now on such images as those named above to fill out their meaning in the present day. Who is Jesus Christ for us today? How can the church be the church today? What is a plausible and faithful doctrine of the church for today? I have attempted here to offer a number of salient though partial answers to those always important questions.

Epilogue

Poststructuralists and deconstructionists have for some years treated religious, theological language and texts as though they have significance (or do not) apart from the role they play in the life of the church. This is an egregious oversight and error. Narrativists have known, and said, for some time that theological language is the language of a convictional community, and its significance hangs on how it functions in the life of the community of faith. Language about baptism has meaning for people who are baptized. Language about the Lord's Supper has meaning for those who partake the Lord's Supper. For such ones, baptistic and eucharistic language shapes their experience of themselves, the world, and all that is. Interpretation of the Bible is not something which has reality apart from the day-to-day experience of people whose life stories are written and re-written by the Story learned and entered into intratextually through the Bible. It is for that reason that theologians who are asking questions from within the community of faith have only marginal interest in and need for the scholarly yield of various poststructuralists, neopragmatists, deconstructionists, and others currently offering their answers to modernism and its errors. Descendants of Barth, at least in terms of his insistence that dogmatics be *church* dogmatics, narrativists are not principally concerned to answer modernism on other than ecclesial grounds. Their concern is a churchly one. Their questions, then, about the biblical text and its interpretation, and about the nature of theological language, are questions about what these mean for the church. They are questions about what these mean for the church's living out its faith, its defining discipleship. Like Bonhoeffer half a century ago, they know that the central question is still Who is Jesus Christ for us today? Linked inextricably to that question is another: What does it mean for the church to be the church today?

168

The narrative perspective and method I have set forth in this book attempt a credible response to those questions. Jesus' central mission was to invite all the world into God's house, I have argued. Hospitality is at the core of Christology. For that reason, ecclesiology and anthropology are also, at their core, hospitality. Thus, the answer to the preceding question needs to take its departure from that core of hospitality and what it means to follow Jesus in a radical fellowship of the cross which self-sacrificially joins God in issuing the invitation to God's world house and otherworld house.

In this work, I have offered a narrative method which I call *interlacing*, the substance of which is exactly that—interlacing biblical stories and many other stories in the generative context of the faith community's worship and discipleship. I have argued that this is a productive and faithful method for the theologian and, indeed, for the Christian community itself. To be sure, it is the method employed by biblical theologians and evangelists before us and by Christians and churches across the centuries. Now, *we need to adopt this method consciously, intentionally, imaginatively, and responsibly*, I propose.

Such a methodology will need to follow certain clearly defined criteria for going about its task. Some critics have said that narrative theology fails to measure itself by adequate criteria in its scriptural interpretation. That may in some cases be true. If so, hard work needs to be done to revise that situation wherever it might exist.

Accordingly, I propose here a list of criteria to guide the work of interpretation as biblical narratives are interlaced with biographical, autobiographical, literary, and other narratives linked by worship and discipleship. As James McClendon has pointed out, Christians read the Bible with a conscious, intentional bias. That bias is a Christological one. Biblical passages are read in light of the centrality of the Jesus Story and in light of the *whole* of the Story of Jesus. In an essay entitled "Radiance and Obscurity in Biblical Narrative," Ronald Thiemann has offered suggestions for how the Story of Jesus can be centralized in our exegesis (Thiemann, 1987:27–38). With some obscurity of his own, since these suggestions have to be ferreted out carefully by the reader, Thiemann sets forth what I have identified as seven criteria for a *Christologically-biased* exegesis centralizing the Story of Jesus and

169

submitting all biblical interpretation, Hebrew as well as Greek, to those criteria and that conscious, deliberate bias. I think that Thiemann's criteria are workable ones. Those, or others compatible with them, furnish the narrativist with valuable rules, or measuring devices, for negotiating potentially conflicting interpretations as stories are interlaced and ideas emerge. To Thiemann's seven criteria I have added two more; his and mine are as follows:

1. Does the interpretation present a "plausible, followable world"?
2. Does the interpretation convince the reader that the Bible presents "trustworthy promise"?
3. Is the interpretation an extraordinary reading produced by faith, defined as an "act of intellectual and personal commitment based upon a coherent reading of the biblical narratives"?
4. Does the interpretation recognize Jesus as Son of God, "an agent enacting God's saving intentions by identifying with those who live on the margins of society"?
5. Does the interpretation foster "embarking on a journey of self-denial, cross-bearing, and death"?
6. Does the interpretation invite the whole world to respond in faith to God's promise by entering the world of the text and undertaking the journey of discipleship?
7. Does the interpretation enable the continuation of God's story through the faith community? (Thiemann, 1987:27–38)

And to Thiemann's criteria I add:

8. Does the interpretation invite all people into God's house, a hospitable place of "friendly emptiness" where each person can find her or his own work of redemptive justice, peace, and love?
9. Does the interpretation honor the natural creation as setting of God's hospitable world house, valuable to God and to itself, apart from human interests?

I believe that, with the help of these criteria, or others as faithfully Christological, the challenging work of being the Christian church in this contemporary era of poverty, social injustice, spiritual aridity, war, and ecological violence can make the kind of difference the church has been authorized and commissioned by Christ to make. In the preceding pages, I have sought to employ Thiemann's guidelines and my own. What remains to be seen is whether these criteria, and the method I have proposed, have potential and currency for those Christians and Christian congregations reading this text. I believe that they do.

BARNES, Elizabeth
 1987 *An Affront to the Gospel? The Radical Barth and the Southern Baptist Convention.* Atlanta: Scholars Press.

BARTH, Karl
 1936–69 *Church Dogmatics* (4 vols.). Trans. G. T. Thomson, et al. Edinburgh: T & T Clark.

 1956 *The Doctrine of Reconciliation* (*Church Dogmatics,* IV/I). Trans. G. W. Bromiley. Edinburgh: T & T Clark.

BAUSCH, William J.
 1984 *Storytelling: Imagination and Faith.* Mystic, Conn.: Twenty-Third Publications.

BONHOEFFER, Dietrich
 1937/1959 *The Cost of Discipleship.* Trans. R. H. Fuller, with Irmgard Booth. London: SCM Press.

 1938/1954 *Life Together.* Trans. with Intro. by John W. Doberstein. San Francisco: Harper & Row.

 1953/1979 *Letters and Papers from Prison,* enlarged ed. Trans. R. H. Fuller, et al., and ed. Eberhard Bethge. New York: Macmillan Publishing Co.

CROSSAN, John Dominic
 1975 *The Dark Interval: Towards a Theology of Story* Niles, Ill.: Argus Communications.

DINESEN, Isak

1937, 1960/ *Out of Africa and Shadows on the Grass.* New
1985   York: Vintage Books.

1953/1988   *Babette's Feast and Other Anecdotes of Destiny.*
            New York: Vintage Books.

ELIOT, T. S.
1951   "The Love Song of J. Alfred Prufrock" in *Col-
            lected Poems 1909–1935.* London: Faber and
            Faber Limited.

FAULKNER, William
1946/1977   "Address upon Receiving the Nobel Prize for
            Literature" in Malcolm Cowley, ed., *The Port-
            able Faulkner.* New York: Penguin Books.

GADAMER, Hans Georg
1976   *Philosophical Hermeneutics.* Trans. and ed. by
            David E. Linge. Berkeley: University of Cali-
            fornia Press.

HAUERWAS, Stanley
1977   *Truthfulness and Tragedy* (with Richard Bondi
            and David B. Burrell). Notre Dame, Indiana:
            University of Notre Dame Press.

1981   *A Community of Character: Toward A Construc-
            tive Christian Social Ethic.* Notre Dame, Indi-
            ana: University of Notre Dame Press.

HEILBRUN, Carolyn G.
1990   *Hamlet's Mother and Other Women.* New York:
            Columbia University Press.

LINDBECK, George A.
1984   *The Nature of Doctrine: Religion and Theology in
            a Postliberal Age.* Philadelphia: Westminster
            Press.

LUCE, William
1989/1992   *Lucifer's Child: A One-Woman Play Based on the Writings of Isak Dinesen*. New York: Samuel French.

McCLENDON, James Wm., Jr.
1974   *Biography as Theology: How Life Stories Can Remake Today's Theology*. Nashville: Abingdon Press.

1986   *Ethics: Systematic Theology*, Vol. I. Nashville: Abingdon Press.

1994   *Doctrine: Systematic Theology*, Vol. II. Nashville: Abingdon Press.

McFAGUE, Sallie
1975   *Speaking in Parables: A Study in Metaphor and Theology*. London: SCM Press.

MOLTMANN-WENDEL, Elisabeth
1986   *A Land Flowing with Milk and Honey: Perspectives on Feminist Theology*. London: SCM Press.

NOUWEN, Henri J. M.
1975   *Reaching Out: The Three Movements of the Spiritual Life*. Garden City, N. Y.: Doubleday.

O'CONNOR, Flannery
1946/1989   "A Good Man Is Hard to Find" in *The Complete Stories*. New York: The Noonday Press.

RUSSELL, Letty M.
1982   *Becoming Human*. Philadelphia: Westminster Press.

1987   *Household of Freedom: Authority in Feminist Theology*. Philadelphia: Westminster Press.

1993   *Church in the Round: Feminist Interpretation of*

the Church. Louisville: Westminster/John Knox Press.

STEINBECK, John
1939/1976 *The Grapes of Wrath.* New York: Penguin Books.

THIEMANN, Ronald F.
1985/1987 *Revelation and Theology: The Gospel as Narrated Promise.* Notre Dame, Indiana: University of Notre Dame Press.

1987 "Radiance and Obscurity in Biblical Narrative" in Garrett Green, ed., *Scriptural Authority and Narrative Interpretation.* Philadelphia: Fortress Press.

VIA, Dan O., Jr.
1990 *Self-Deception and Wholeness in Paul and Matthew.* Minneapolis: Fortress Press.

VON RAD, Gerhard
1961 *Genesis: A Commentary.* (German, 1956) Trans. John H. Marks. Philadelphia: Westminster Press.

WILLIAMS, Mel.
1991 "How Can Christians Become Christian?", unpublished sermon.

1992 "The Messiah Is Among You," unpublished sermon.

WINGEIER, Douglas E.
1985 *Jesus Christ: Resurrection.* Nashville: Graded Press.